RECORDED VERSIONS GUITAR

ACCURATE TAB EDITION

ED Sheeran
DIVIDE

Music transcriptions by Pete Billmann and Jeff Jacobson

ISBN 978-1-4950-9511-5

HAL•LEONARD®

7777 W. Bluemound Rd. P.O. Box 13819 Milwaukee, WI 53213

In Australia Contact:
Hal Leonard Australia Pty. Ltd.
4 Lentara Court
Cheltenham, Victoria, 3192 Australia
Email: ausadmin@halleonard.com.au

Visit Hal Leonard Online at
www.halleonard.com

Eraser

Words and Music by Ed Sheeran and Johnny McDaid

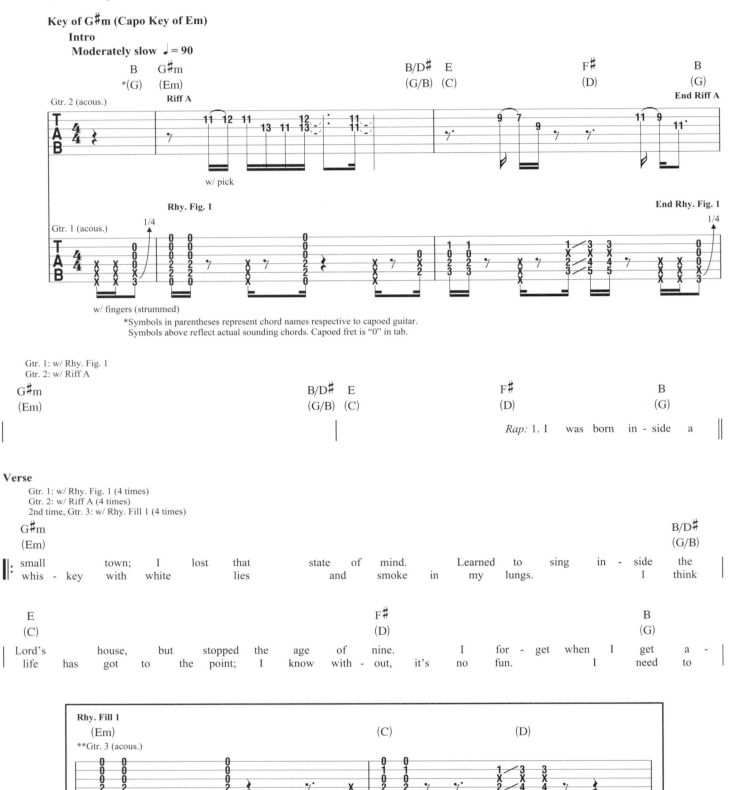

*Symbols in parentheses represent chord names respective to capoed guitar.
Symbols above reflect actual sounding chords. Capoed fret is "0" in tab.

G#m (Em)								B/D# (G/B)

wards   now, the   wave   I   had   to   ride,   the   pav - ing stones I
get   in   the   right   mind   and   clear my - self up.   In - stead,   I

E (C)   **F# (D)**   **B (G)**

played up - on that kept me on the grind.   So blame it on the
look in the mir - ror; ques - tion - ing what I've be - come.   Guess it's a

G#m (Em)   **B/D# (G/B)**

pain   that blessed me   with the life,   friends and fam - i - ly filled with
ster - e - o - typ - i - cal day for some - one like me,   with - out a

E (C)   **F# (D)**   **B (G)**

en - vy when they should be filled with pride.   And when the world's a -
nine - to - five job or a u - ni de - gree.   To be

G#m (Em)   **B/D# (G/B)**

gainst me is when I real - ly come a - live. And ev - 'ry day that Sa - tan
caught up in the trap - pings of the in - dus - try. Show me the

1.

E (C)   **F# (D)**   **B (G)**

tempts me, I try to take it in my stride.   2. You know that I've got

2.

E (C)   **F# (D)**   **B (G)**

locked doors, I'll find an - oth - er use for the key.   And you'll see...

𝄉 Pre-Chorus

Sung: I'm well a - ware of cer - tain things { that can de-stroy / that will be - fall } a man like me.

Eadd9 (C)   **B5 (G)**   **F# (D5)**   **C#m7 (A7sus4)**

Gtr. 1
let ring — let ring — sim.

*Gtr. 4 (acous.)
let ring —
P.M. — P.M. — P.M. — P.M. — P.M.
*Two gtrs. arr. for one.

5

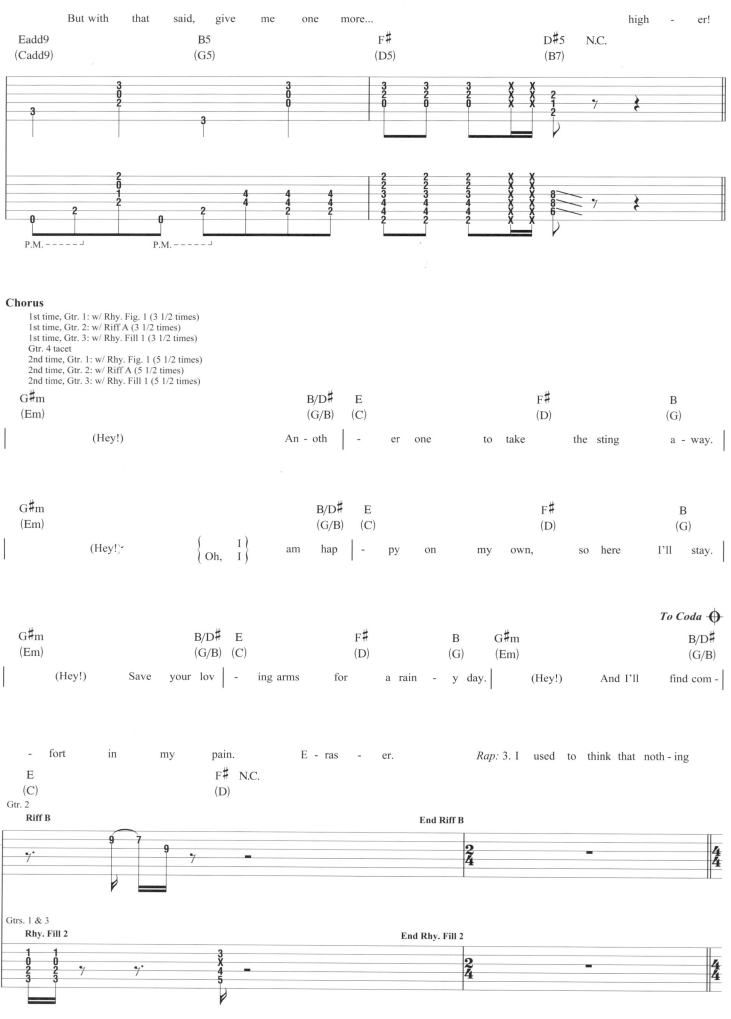

Verse

Gtr. 1: w/ Rhy. Fig. 1 (3 1/2 times)
Gtr. 2: w/ Riff A (3 1/2 times)
Gtr. 3: w/ Rhy. Fill 1 (3 1/2 times)

G#m
(Em)   B/D#
                                                                                                                       (G/B)
could   be   bet - ter   than   tour - ing   the   world   with   my   songs.   I   chased   the
sa - tions with   my   fath - er   on   the   A - Four - teen,   age

E
(C)   F#   B
                                                             (D)   (G)
pic - ture - per - fect life;   I   think   they   paint - ed   it   wrong.   I   think   that
twelve,   tell - in'   me   I've   got - ta   chase   those   dreams.   Now   I'm

G#m
(Em)   B/D#
                                                                                                                       (G/B)
mon - ey   is   the   root   of   all   e - vil,   and   fame   is   hell.   Re -
play - ing   for   the   peo - ple,   Dad,   and   they   know   me,   with   my

E
(C)   F#   B
                                                             (D)   (G)
la - tion - ships   and   hearts   you   fix,   they   break   as   well.   And
beat - en,   small   gui - tar,   wear - ing   the   same   old   jeans.   Wem - bl - ey

G#m
(Em)   B/D#
                                                                                                                       (G/B)
ain't   no - bod - y   wan - na   see   you   down   in   the   dumps,   be - cause   you're
Sta - di - um   crowds,   two   hun - dred   and   for - ty   thou.   I   may   have

E
(C)   F#   B
                                                             (D)   (G)
liv - ing   your   dream,   man,   it   should   be   fun.   Please   know   that
grown   up,   but   I   hope   that   Da - mi - en's   proud.   And   to   the

G#m
(Em)   B/D#
                                                                                                                       (G/B)
I'm   not   try'n'   to   preach   like   I'm   Rev - er - end   Run.   I   beg   you,
next   gen - er - a - tion,   in - spi - ra - tion's   al - lowed.   The   world   may

1.

Gtrs. 1 & 3: w/ Rhy. Fill 2
Gtr. 2: w/ Riff B

E
(C)   F#   N.C.
                                                             (D)
don't   be   dis - ap - point - ed   with   the   man   I've   be - come.   4. Old   con - ver -

2.

D.S. al Coda

Gtr. 2: w/ Riff B
Gtr. 3: w/ Rhy. Fill 2

be   filled   with   hate,   but   keep   e - ras - ing   it   now,   some - how.

E   F#   N.C.
(C)   (D)

Gtr. 1

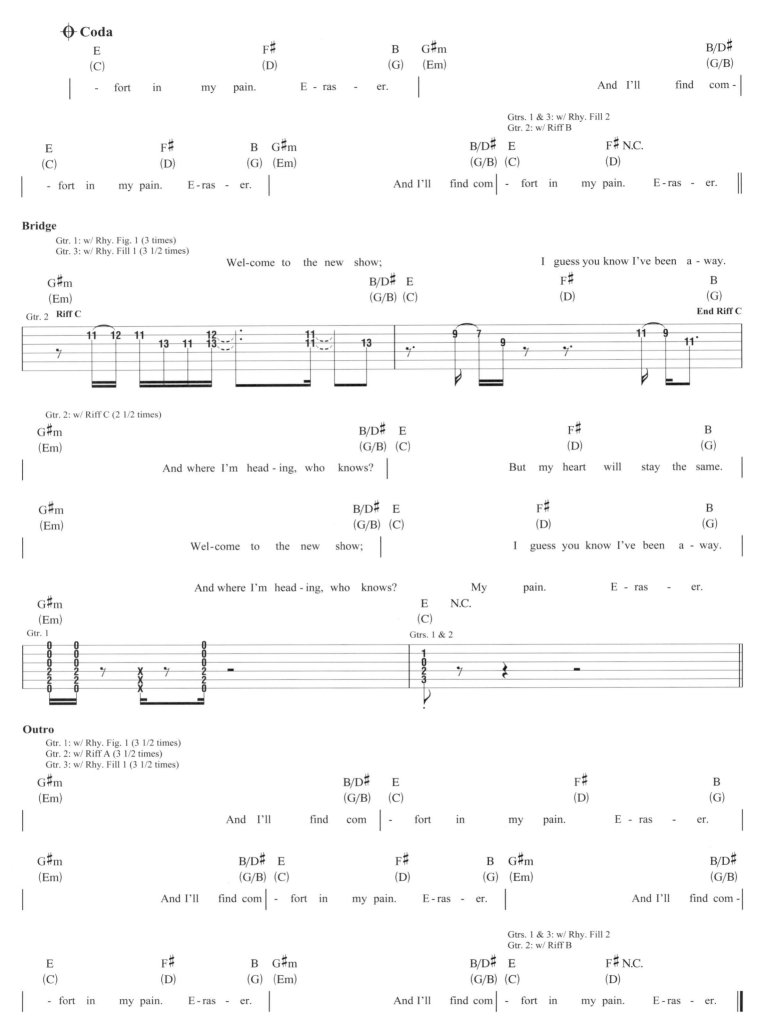

8

Castle on the Hill

Words and Music by Ed Sheeran and Benjamin Levin

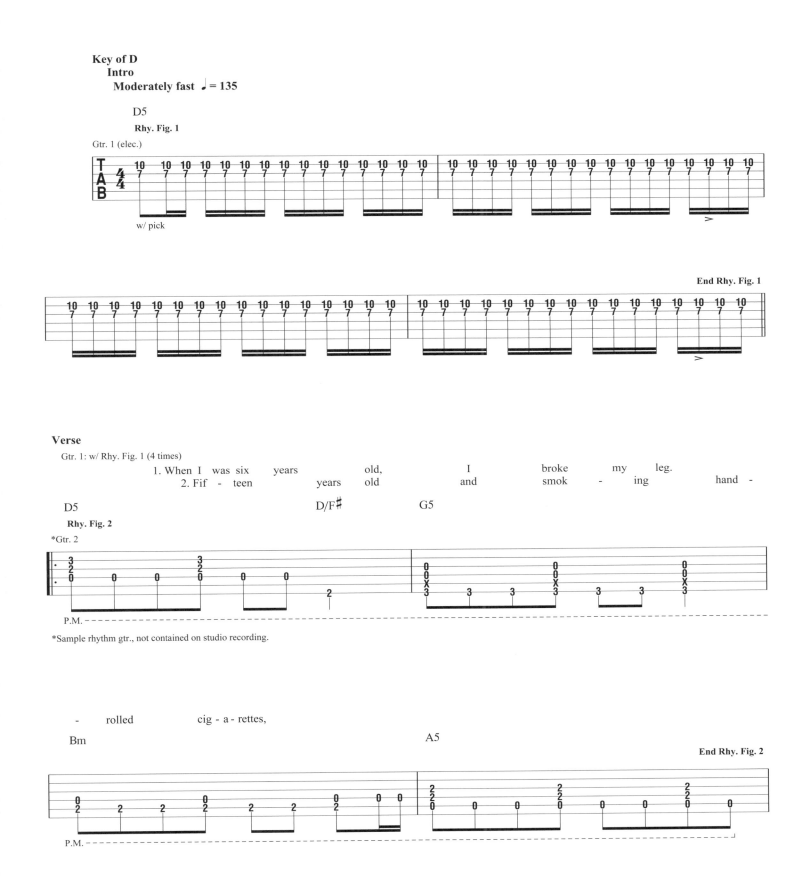

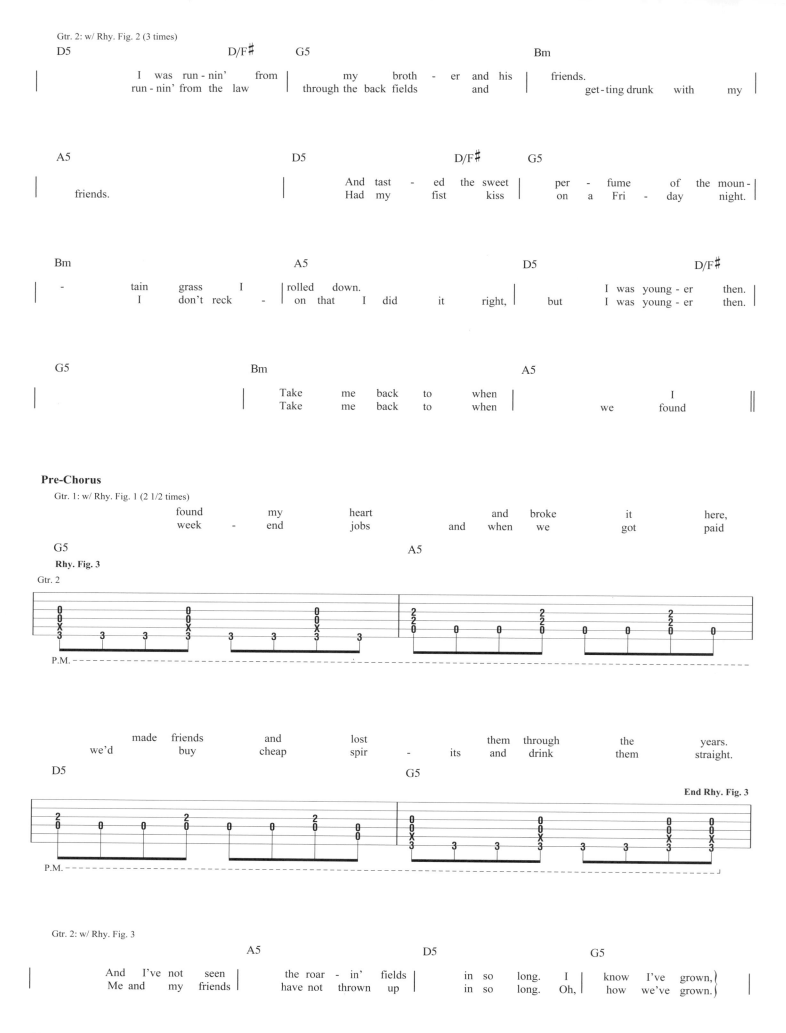

Gtr. 2: w/ Rhy. Fig. 2 (3 times)

D5   D/F#   G5   Bm

I was run-nin' from   my   broth - er and his   friends.
run - nin' from the law   through the back fields   and   get-ting drunk with   my

A5   D5   D/F#   G5

friends.   And   tast - ed the sweet   per - fume   of the moun -
                         Had my   fist   kiss   on   a   Fri - day   night.

Bm   A5   D5   D/F#

- tain   grass   I   rolled   down.   I was young - er   then.
     I   don't reck -   on that   I   did   it   right,   but   I was young - er   then.

G5   Bm   A5

Take   me   back   to   when   I
Take   me   back   to   when   we   found

Pre-Chorus

Gtr. 1: w/ Rhy. Fig. 1 (2 1/2 times)

found   my   heart   and   broke   it   here,
week - end   jobs   and   when   we   it   got   here, paid

G5   A5

Rhy. Fig. 3

Gtr. 2

P.M. -

made   friends   and   lost   them through   the   years.
we'd   buy   cheap   spir -   its   and   drink   them   straight.

D5   G5   **End Rhy. Fig. 3**

P.M. -

Gtr. 2: w/ Rhy. Fig. 3

A5   D5   G5

And   I've not   seen   the roar - in' fields   in so   long.   I   know I've grown, ⎱
Me and   my friends   have not thrown up   in so   long. Oh,   how   we've grown. ⎰

but I can't wait to go home.

A5

Gtr. 2

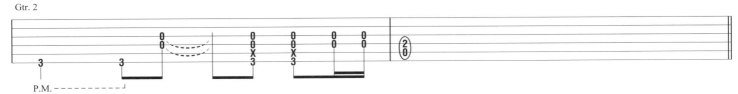

P.M. - - - - - - - - - ┘

Chorus

Gtr. 1: w/ Rhy. Fig. 1 (4 times)

I'm on my way, driv - in' at nine - ty down those

D   D/F♯   G5   Bm7   A7sus4

                       End Rhy. Fig. 4

Gtr. 2

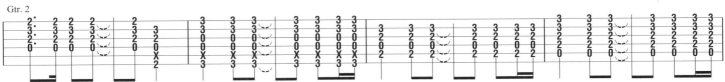

Gtr. 2: w/ Rhy. Fig. 4 (3 times)

D   D/F♯   G5   Bm7   A7sus4

| coun - try lanes, | sing - in' to "Ti | - ny Danc - er." And |

D   D/F♯   G5   Bm7   A7sus4

| I miss the way | you made | me feel, | and it's real, when |

D   D/F♯   G5   Bm7   A7sus4

| we watched the sun | set o | - ver the cas | - tle on the hill. ‖

1.

Interlude

Gtr. 1: w/ Rhy. Fig. 1 (1st 2 meas.)

D

Gtr. 2

2.

Interlude

Gtr. 1: w/ Rhy. Fig. 1 (2 times)
Gtr. 2: w/ Rhy. Fig. 4 (2 times)

D   D/F♯   G5   Bm7   A7sus4

| Hee, hoo, | o | - ver the cas | - tle on the hill. |

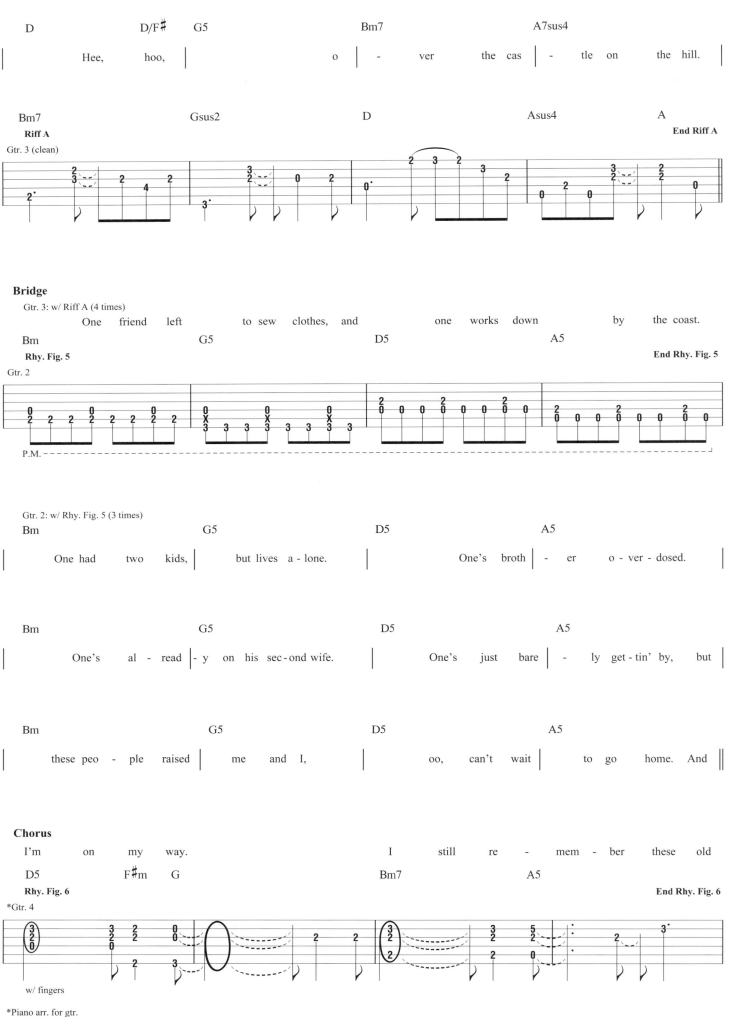

Bridge

Chorus

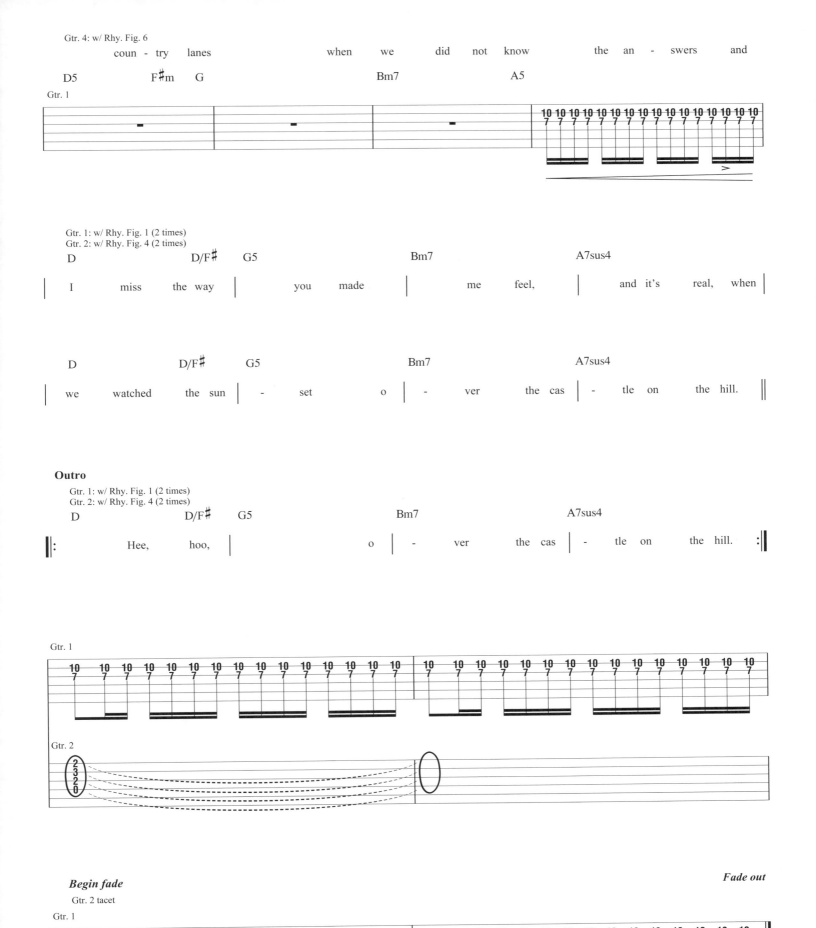

Dive

Words and Music by Ed Sheeran, Benjamin Levin and Julia Michaels

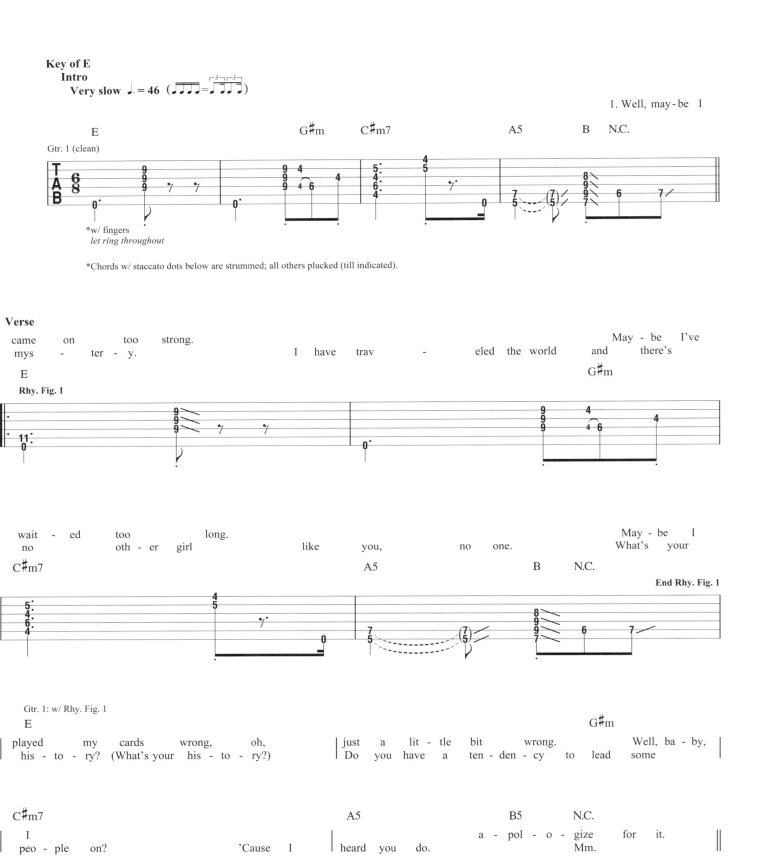

Pre-Chorus

*Strum all chords (next 2 meas.).

*Strum chords throughout Chorus.

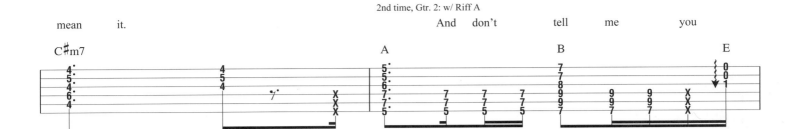

mean   it.

And   don't   tell   me   you

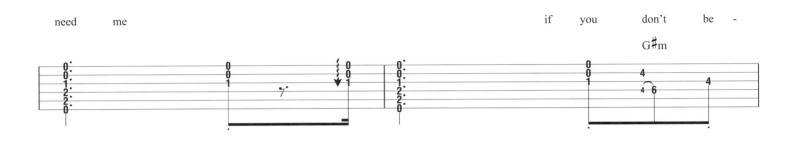

need   me

if   you   don't   be -

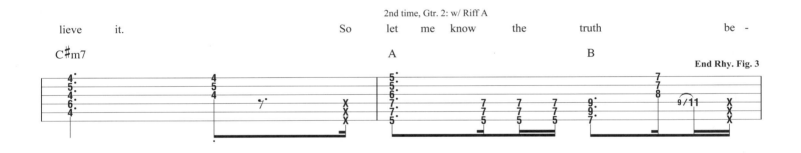

lieve   it.

So   let   me   know   the   truth   be -

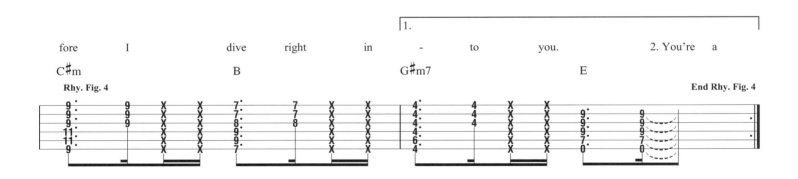

fore   I   dive   right   in - to   you.

2. You're   a

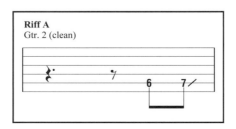

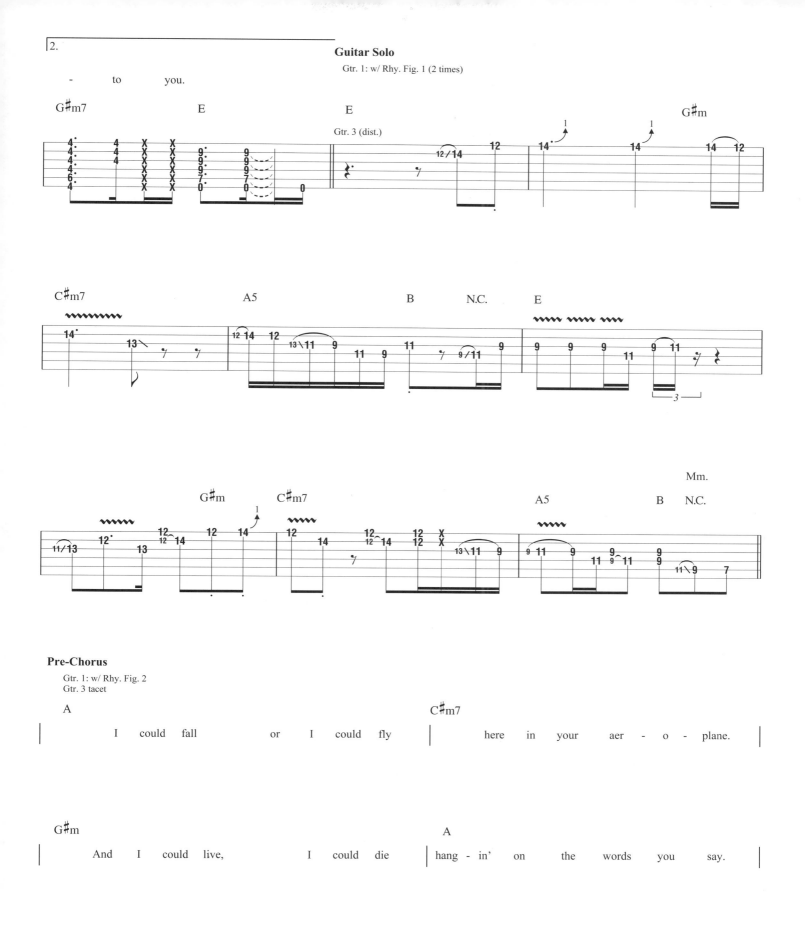

Guitar Solo

Gtr. 1: w/ Rhy. Fig. 1 (2 times)

Pre-Chorus

Gtr. 1: w/ Rhy. Fig. 2
Gtr. 3 tacet

A
  I could fall   or I could fly   C#m7 here in your aer - o - plane.

G#m
  And I could live, I could die A hang - in' on the words you say.

  And I've been known to give my all C#m7 and sit - tin' back, look - in' at

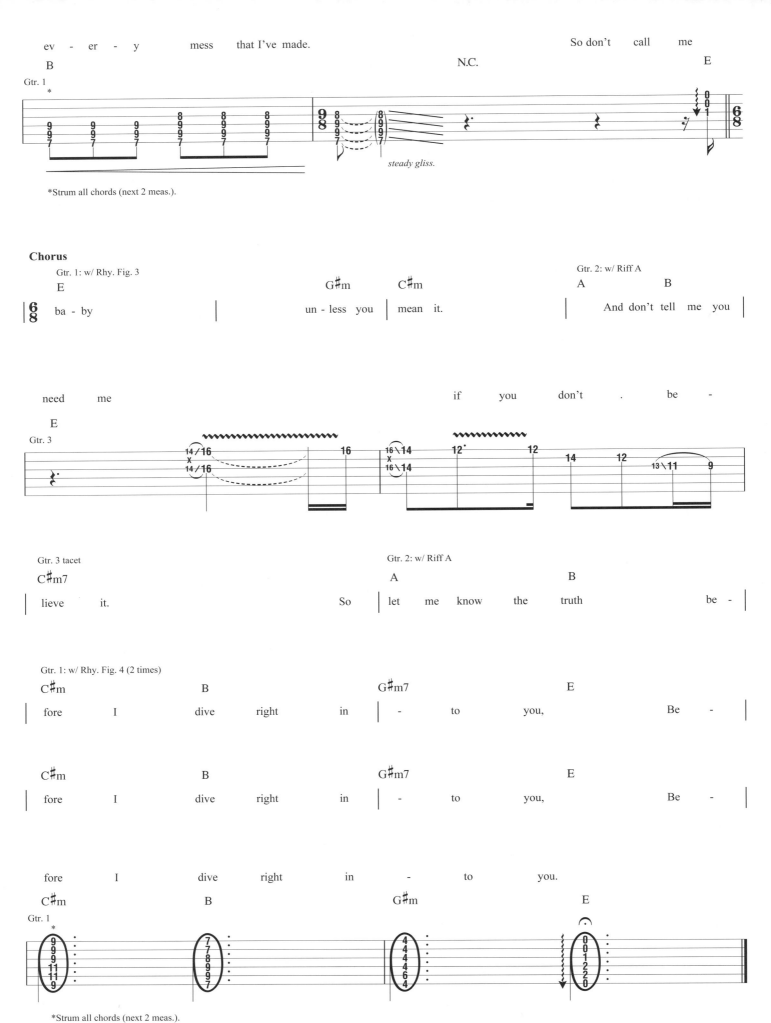

Shape of You

Words and Music by Ed Sheeran, Kevin Briggs, Kandi Burruss, Tameka Cottle, Steve Mac and Johnny McDaid

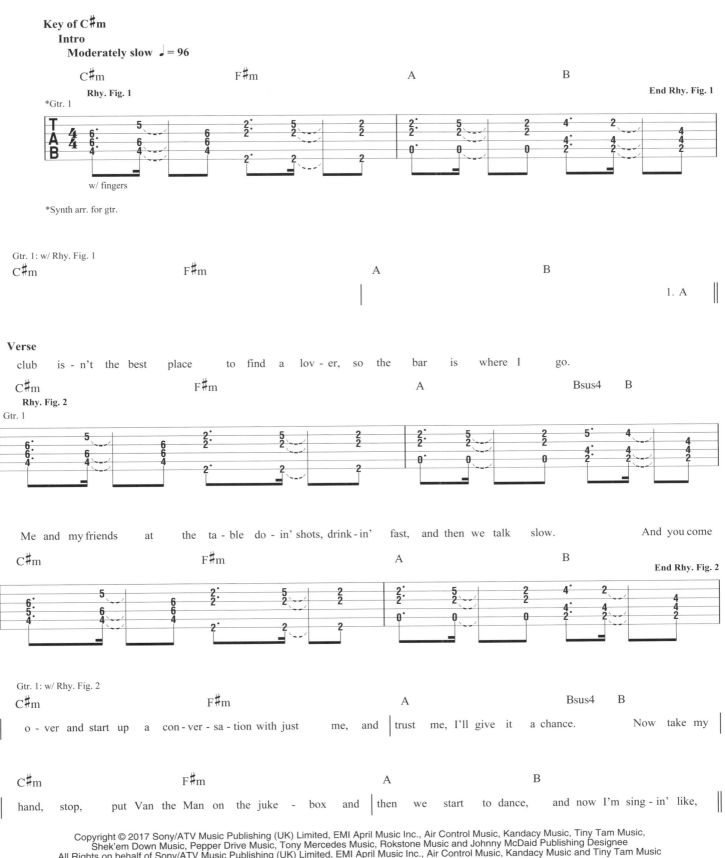

Pre-Chorus

Gtr. 1: w/ Rhy. Fig. 2 (1 1/2 times)

C#m	F#m	A	Bsus4 B
"Girl, you know I want your love.		Your love was hand - made for some - bod - y like	

C#m	F#m	A	B
me. Come on, now, fol - low my lead.		I may be cra - zy, don't mind me. Say	

C#m	F#m	A	Bsus4 B
'Boy, let's not talk too much.		Grab on my waist and put that bod - y on	

me.' Come on, now, fol - low my lead. Come, come on, now, fol - low my lead." Mm.

C#m	F#m	A	N.C.

Rhy. Fig. 3   **End Rhy. Fig. 3**

Gtr. 1

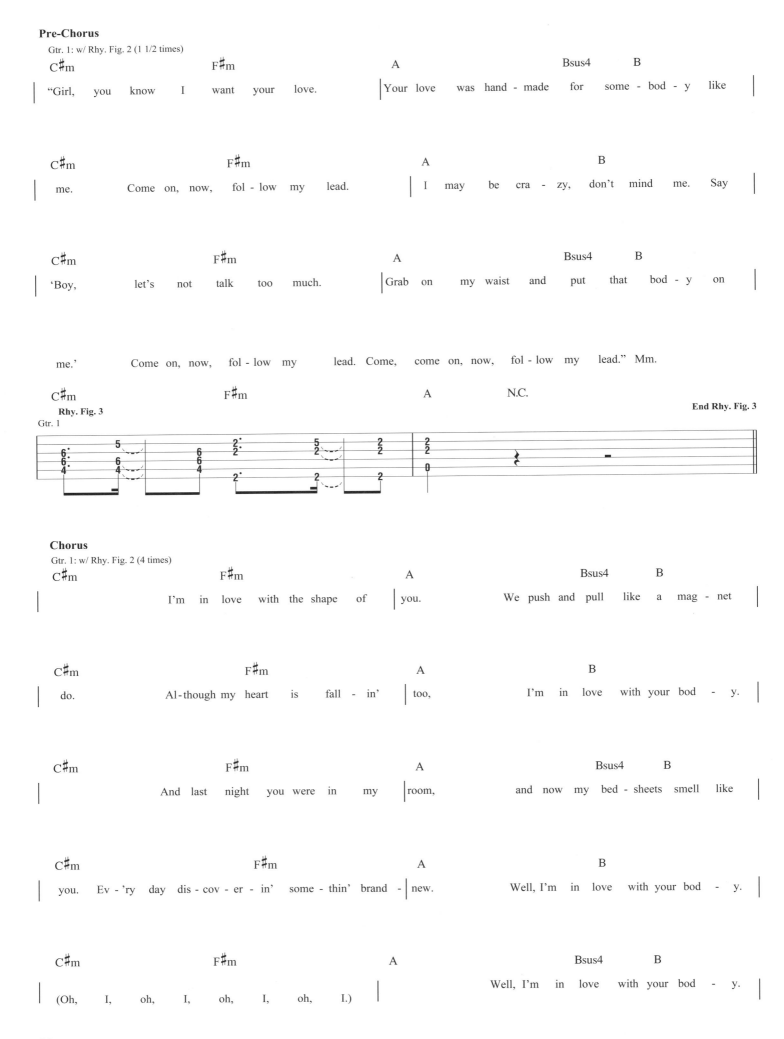

Chorus

Gtr. 1: w/ Rhy. Fig. 2 (4 times)

C#m	F#m	A	Bsus4 B
I'm in love with the shape of	you.	We push and pull like a mag - net	

C#m	F#m	A	B
do. Al-though my heart is fall - in'	too,	I'm in love with your bod - y.	

C#m	F#m	A	Bsus4 B
And last night you were in my	room,	and now my bed - sheets smell like	

C#m	F#m	A	B
you. Ev - 'ry day dis - cov - er - in' some - thin' brand -	new.	Well, I'm in love with your bod - y.	

C#m	F#m	A	Bsus4 B
(Oh, I, oh, I, oh, I, oh, I.)		Well, I'm in love with your bod - y.	

| C#m | F#m | A | B |

(Oh, I, oh, I, oh, I, oh, I.)   Well, I'm in love with your bod - y.

| C#m | F#m | A | Bsus4   B |

(Oh, I, oh, I, oh, I, oh, I.)   Well, I'm in love with your bod - y.

| C#m | F#m | A | B |

Ev -'ry day dis-cov-er - in' some - thin' brand - new.   I'm in love with the shape of

Verse

Gtr. 1: w/ Rhy. Fig. 2 (1st 2 meas.)

| C#m | F#m | A | Bsus4   B |

2. One week in, we let the sto - ry be - gin. We're go - in' | out on our first date.   Well, you and

you.

me are thrift - y, so go "all you can eat," fill up your bag and I fill up a plate.   We talk for

| C#m | F#m | A | N.C. |

Gtr. 1

Gtr. 1: w/ Rhy. Fig. 2

| C#m | F#m | A | Bsus4   B |

hours and hours a - bout sweet and the sour and how your | fam - i - ly is do - in' o - kay.   And leave and

| C#m | F#m | A | B |

get in the tax - i, then kiss in the back - seat. Tell the | driv - er, "Make the ra - di - o play." And I'm sing - in' like,

Pre-Chorus

Gtr. 1: w/ Rhy. Fig. 2 (1 1/2 times)

| C#m | F#m | A | Bsus4   B |

"Girl, you know I want your love. | Your love was hand - made for some - bod - y like

| C#m | F#m | A | B |

me. Come on, now, fol - low my lead. | I may be cra - zy, don't mind me. Say

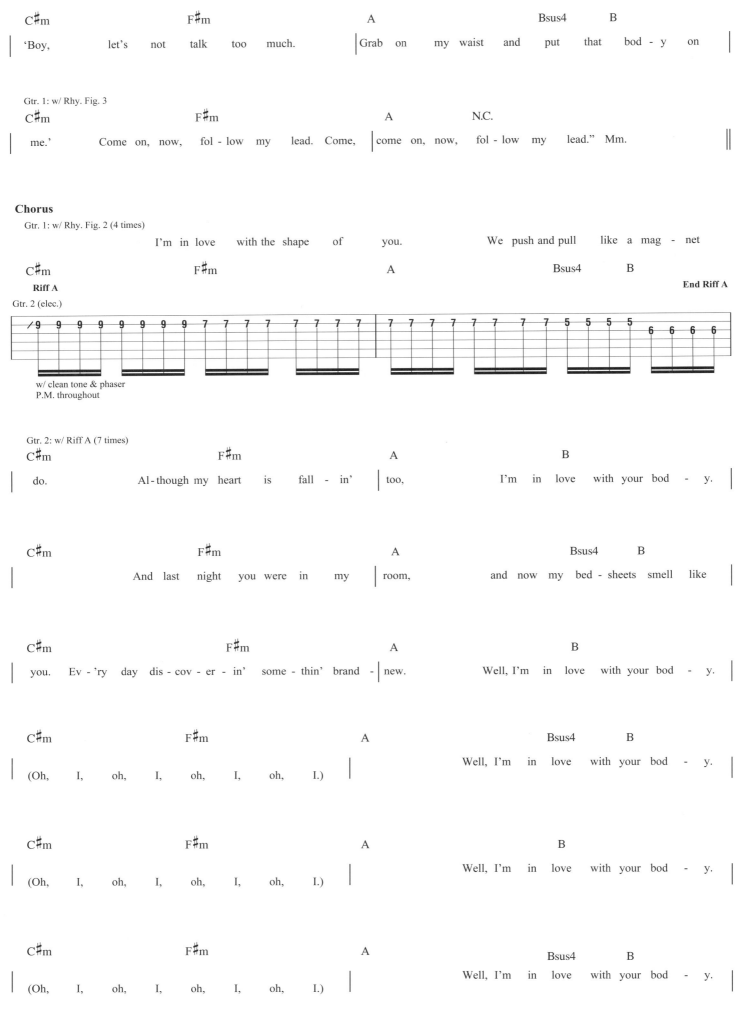

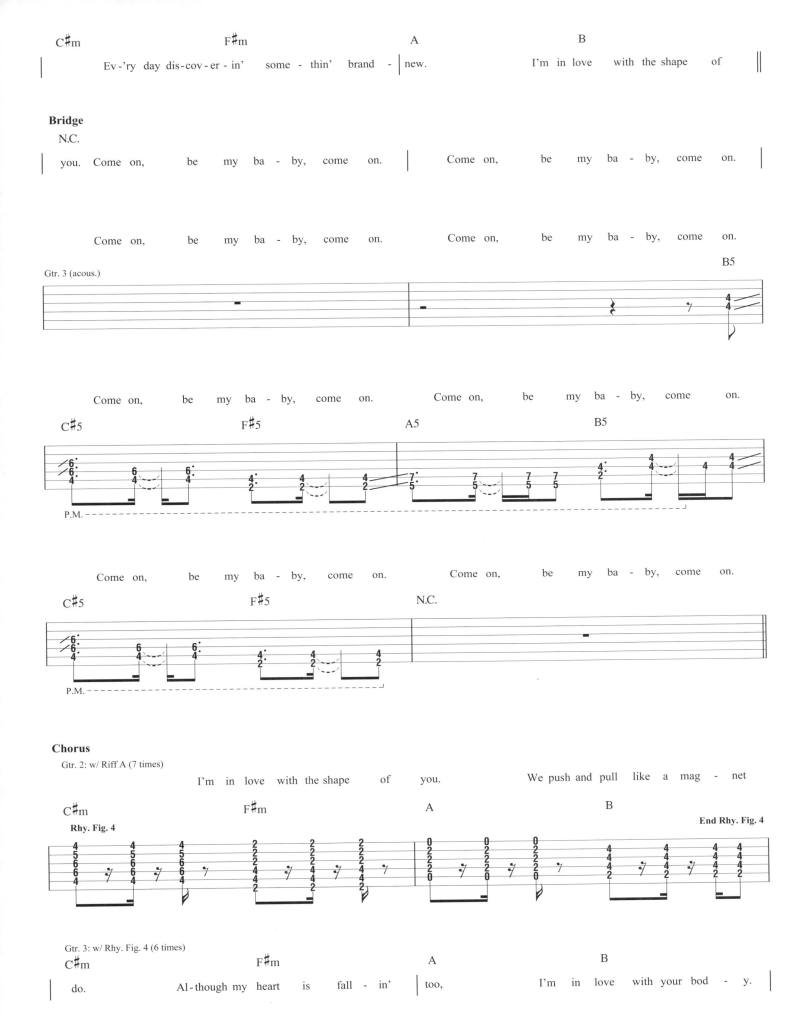

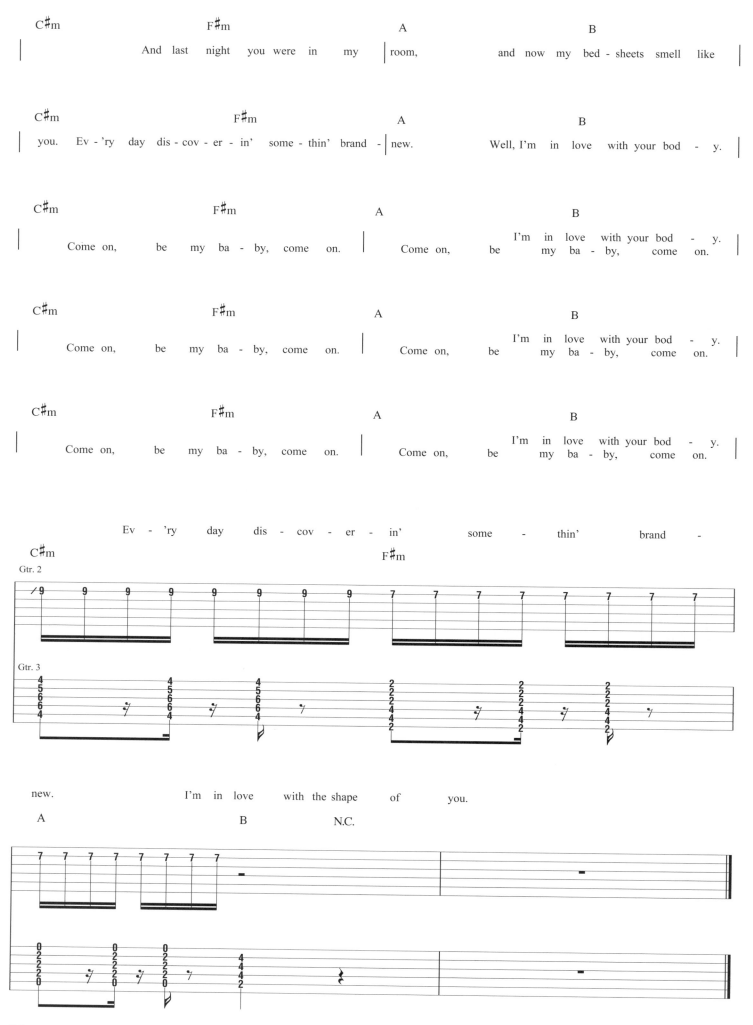

Perfect

Words and Music by Ed Sheeran

Gtr. 1: Capo I

Key of A♭ (Capo Key of G)

Verse

Slow ♩. = 66

1. I found a love   for me.   Dar-ling, just

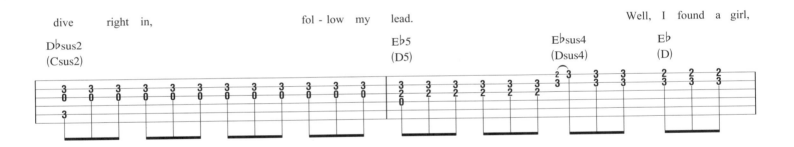

w/ fingers   *let ring throughout*

*1st chord is organ arr. for gtr.

**Symbols in parentheses represent chord names respective to capoed guitar.
Symbols above reflect actual sounding chord. Capoed fret is "0" in tab.

dive right in,   fol - low my lead.   Well, I found a girl,

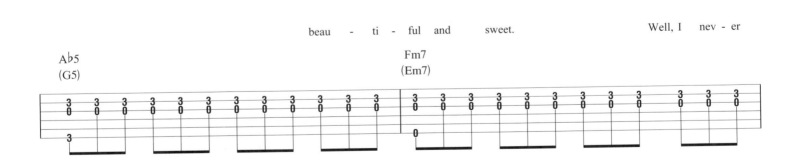

beau - ti - ful and sweet.   Well, I nev - er

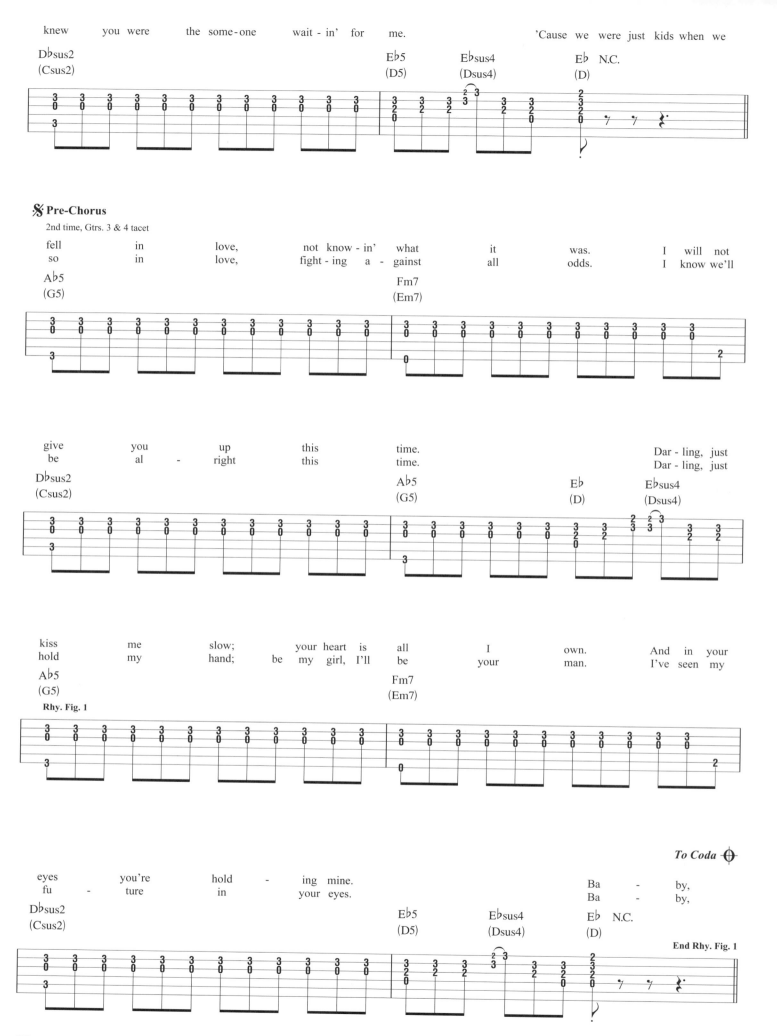

Chorus

I'm danc - ing in the dark with you be - tween my

Fm7 / Db sus2 / Ab5 / Eb / Eb sus4
(Em7) / (Csus2) / (G5) / (D) / (Dsus4)

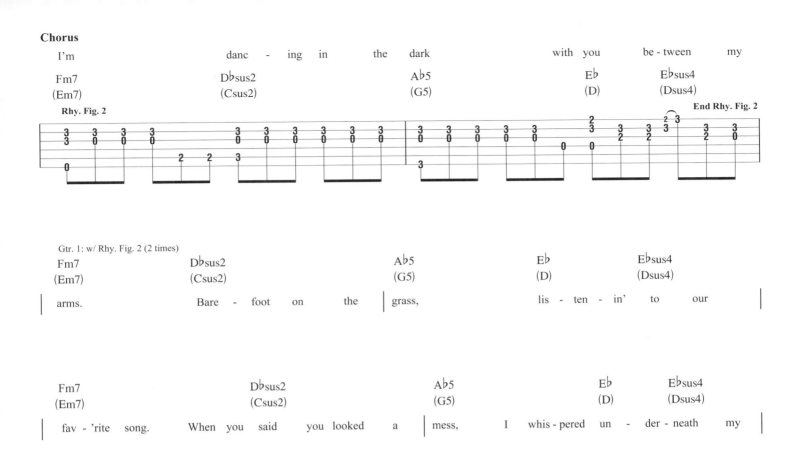

Gtr. 1: w/ Rhy. Fig. 2 (2 times)

Fm7 / Db sus2 / Ab5 / Eb / Eb sus4
(Em7) / (Csus2) / (G5) / (D) / (Dsus4)

arms. Bare - foot on the grass, lis - ten - in' to our

Fm7 / Db sus2 / Ab5 / Eb / Eb sus4
(Em7) / (Csus2) / (G5) / (D) / (Dsus4)

fav - 'rite song. When you said you looked a mess, I whis - pered un - der - neath my

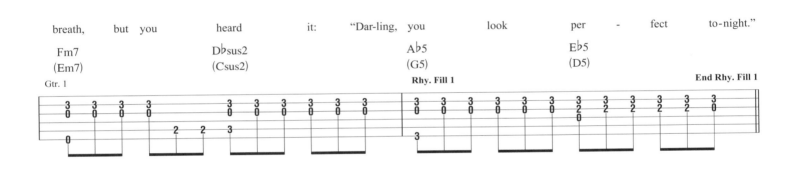

breath, but you heard it: "Dar - ling, you look per - fect to - night."

Fm7 / Db sus2 / Ab5 / Eb5
(Em7) / (Csus2) / (G5) / (D5)

Gtr. 1

Interlude

2. Well, I found a

Ab / Eb/G / Fm7 / Eb / Db / Eb5
(G) / (D/F#) / (Em7) / (D) / (C) / (D5)

Gtr. 2 (acous.)

let ring / let ring / let ring / let ring / let ring

Gtr. 1

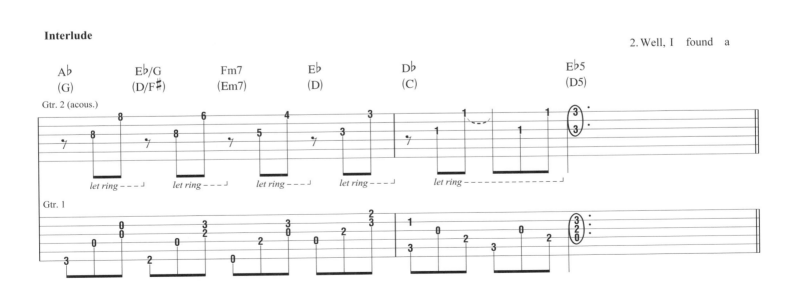

Verse

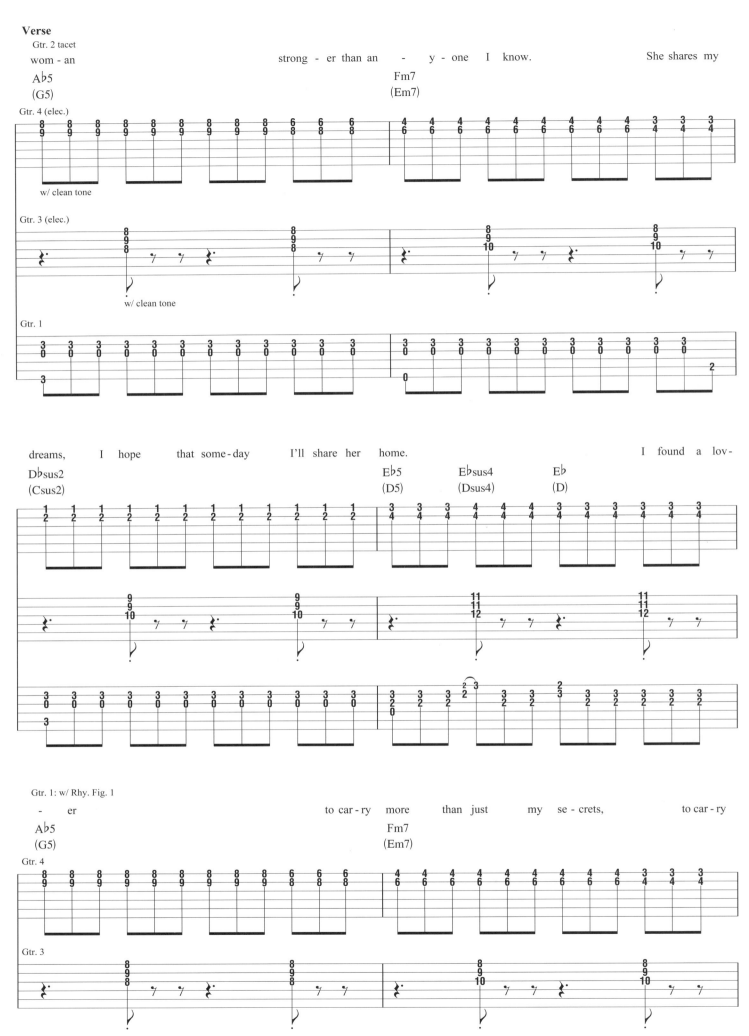

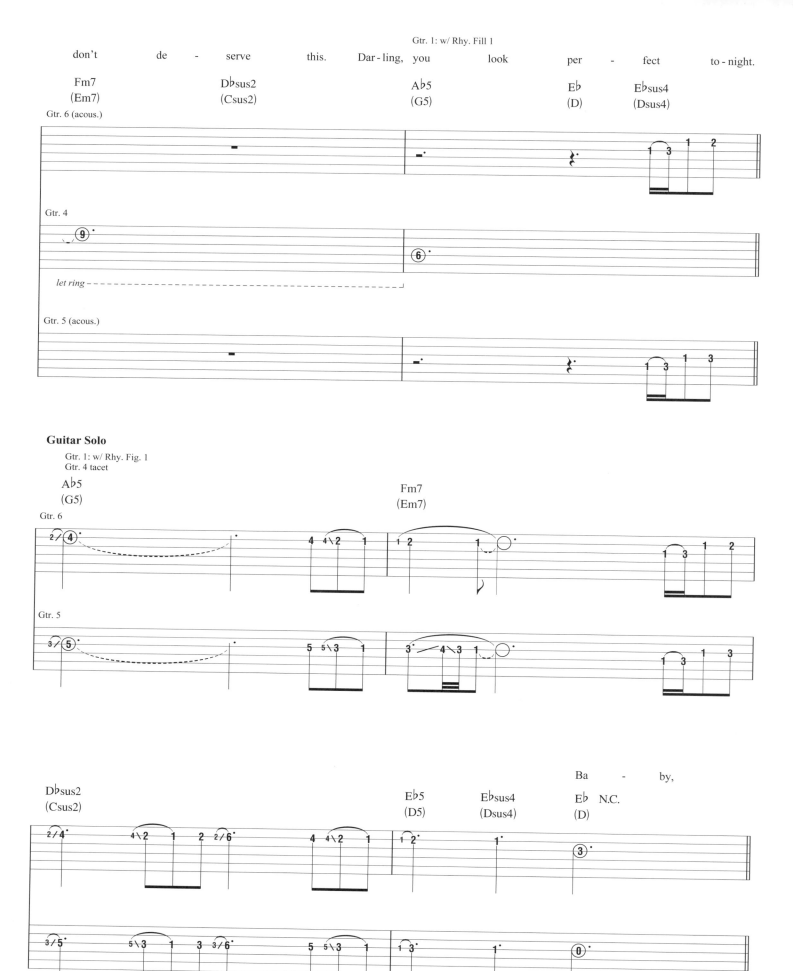

Chorus

Gtr. 1: w/ Rhy. Fig. 2
Gtr. 3: w/ Rhy. Fig. 3 (4 times)

Gtr. 4: w/ Riff A (2 1/2 times)

Fm7	D♭sus2	Ab5	Eb	Ebsus4	Fm7	D♭sus2
(Em7)	(Csus2)	(G5)	(D)	(Dsus4)	(Em7)	(Csus2)

I'm danc - ing in the dark with you be - tween my arms. Bare - foot on the

Ab5	Eb	Ebsus4	Fm7	D♭sus2	Ab5	Eb	Ebsus4
(G5)	(D)	(Dsus4)	(Em7)	(Csus2)	(G5)	(D)	(Dsus4)

grass, lis - ten-ing to our fav-'rite song. I have faith in what I see, now I know I have met an

an - gel in per - son, and she looks per - fect. I

Fm7	D♭sus2	Ab5	Eb	Ebsus4
(Em7)	(Csus2)	(G5)	(D)	(Dsus4)

Gtr. 4

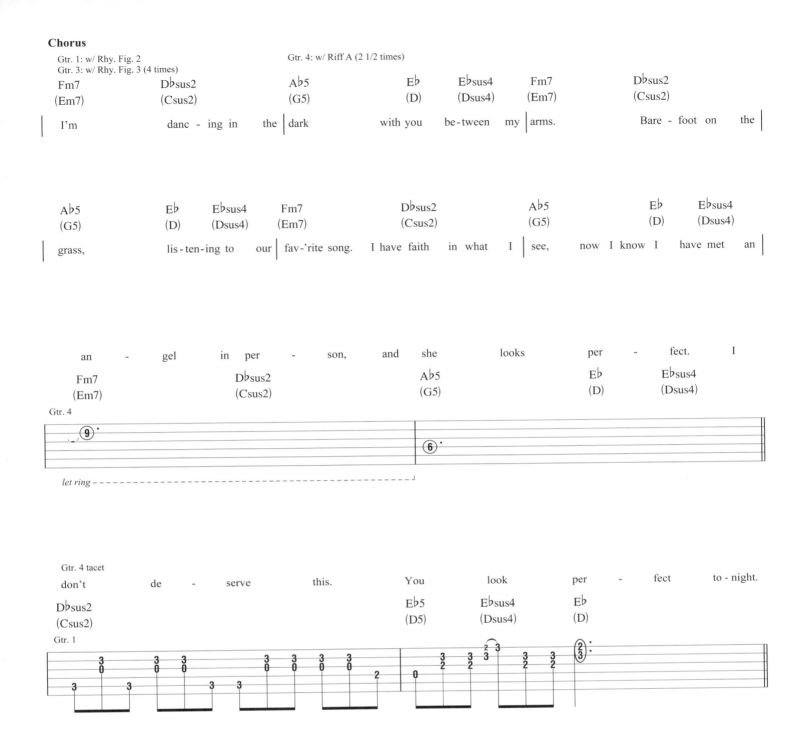

let ring -

Gtr. 4 tacet

don't de - serve this. You look per - fect to - night.

D♭sus2	Eb5	Ebsus4	Eb
(Csus2)	(D5)	(Dsus4)	(D)

Gtr. 1

Outro

Ab	Eb/G	Fm7	Eb	D♭add9	Eb	Ab
(G)	(D/F♯)	(Em7)	(D)	(Cadd9)	(D)	(G)

Gtr. 3

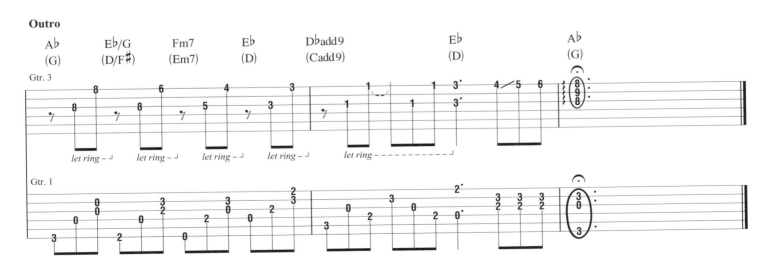

let ring – ⅃   let ring – ⅃   let ring – ⅃   let ring – ⅃   let ring - - - - - - - - - - ⅃

Gtr. 1

Galway Girl

**Words and Music by Ed Sheeran, Foy Vance, Johnny McDaid, Amy Wadge,
Eamon Murray, Niamh Dunne, Liam Bradley, Damian McKee and Sean Graham**

Capo II

Key of A (Capo Key of G)
Pre-Chorus
    Moderately ♩ = 102

She played the fid-dle in an I-rish band, but she fell in love with an En-glish-man. Kissed

F#m   A5   E   Dadd9
*(Em)   (G5)   (D)   (Cadd9)

Gtr. 1 (acous.)

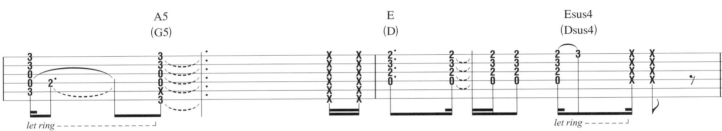

w/ fingers (strummed)   let ring - - - - - - - - - - - - - - - - -

*Symbols in parentheses represent chord names respective to capoed guitar.
Symbols above reflect actual sounding chords. Capoed fret is "0" in tab.

her on the neck and then I took her by the hand, said, "Ba - by, I just wan-na dance." *Rap:* 1. I met her on

     A5   E   Esus4
     (G5)   (D)   (Dsus4)

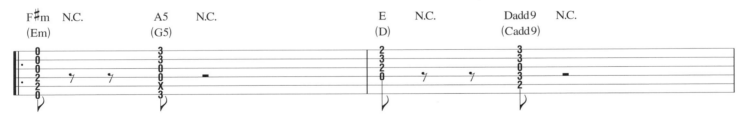

let ring - - - - - - - - - - - - - - - - ┘   let ring - - - - - - ┘

Verse

2nd time, Gtr. 2: w/ Fill 1

Graf-ton Street, right out-side of the bar; she shared a cig-a-rette with me while her broth-er played the gui-tar. She asked me
beat me at darts and then she beat me at pool, and then she kissed me like there was no-bod-y else in the room. At last

F#m   N.C.   A5   N.C.   E   N.C.   Dadd9   N.C.
(Em)   (G5)   (D)   (Cadd9)

Fill 1
Gtr. 2

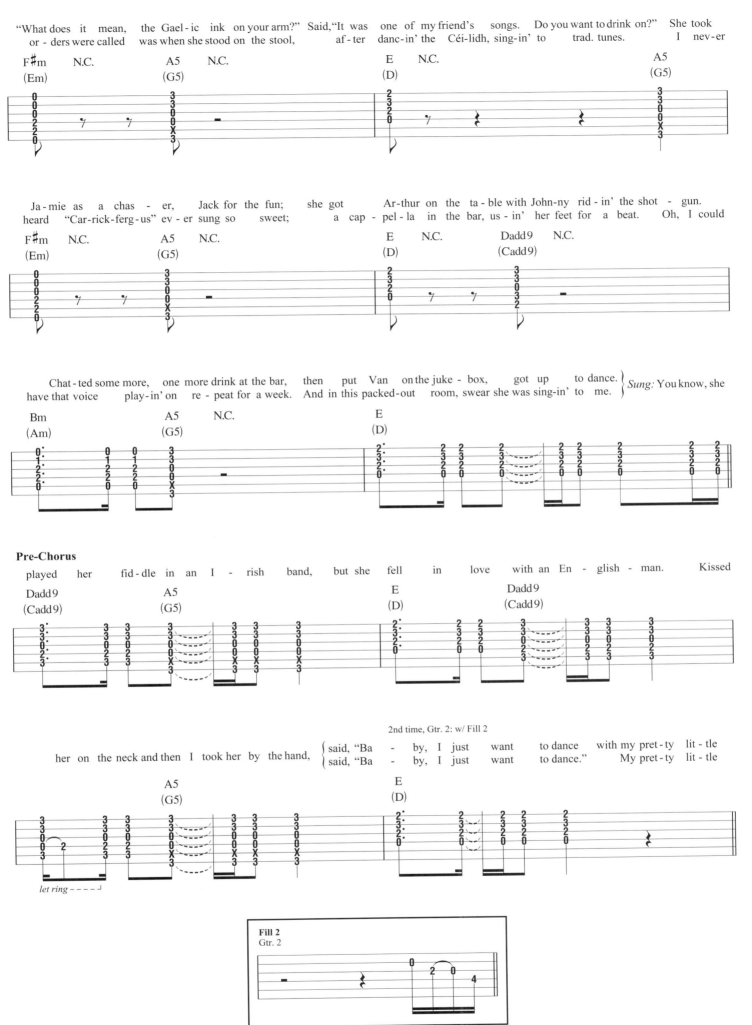

Pre-Chorus

2nd time, Gtr. 2: w/ Fill 2

let ring - - - - ⌐

Fill 2
Gtr. 2

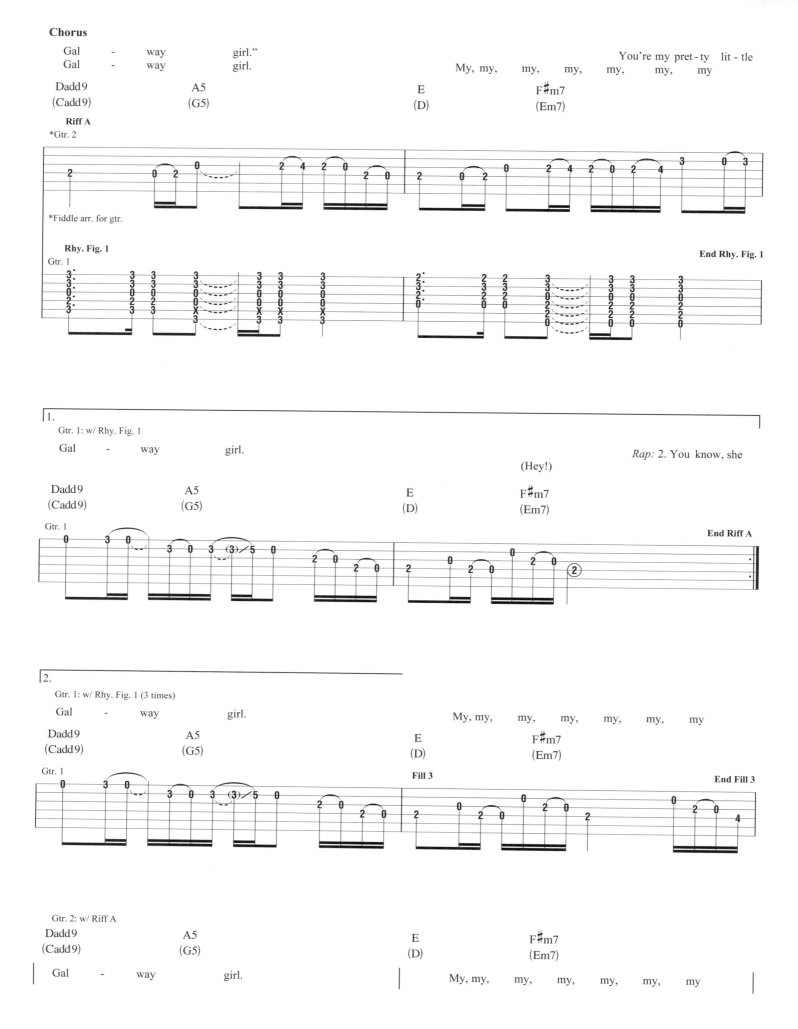

Dadd9 (Cadd9)　　　A5 (G5)　　　　　　　　　　E (D)　　　F#m7 (Em7)

Gal - way　girl.　　　　　　　　　　　　　　　3. And now we've

Verse

Gtr. 2: w/ Fill 1　　　　　　　　　　　　　Gtr. 1 tacet

out - stayed our wel-come and it's clos-in' time;　I was　hold-in' her hand, her hand was hold-in'　mine.　Our

F#m (Em)　　　　　A (G)　　　　　　　E (D)　　　D (C)

Rhy. Fig. 2　　　　　　　　　　　　　　　　End Rhy. Fig. 2

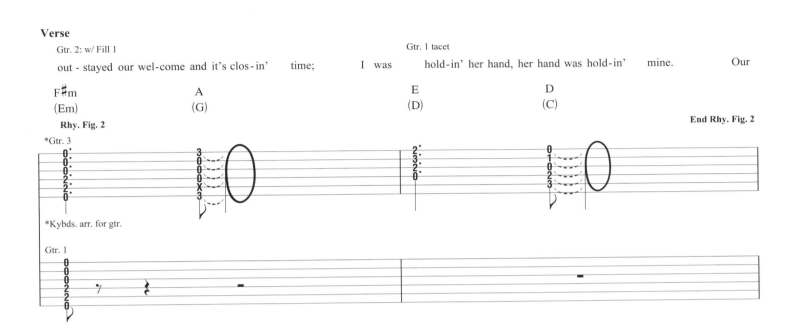

*Gtr. 3

*Kybds. arr. for gtr.

Gtr. 1

coats　both　smell of smoke, whis-key and wine,　as we　fill up our lungs　with the cold　air of the night.　I

F#m (Em)　　　　　A (G)　　　　　　　E (D)

Gtr. 3

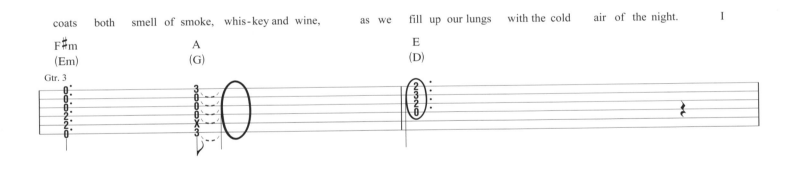

Gtr. 3: w/ Rhy. Fig. 2 (1 1/2 times)

walked　her home,　then she took me in-side　to fin-ish　some Dor - i - tos and an-oth-er bot-tle of wine.　"I

F#m (Em)　　　　　A (G)　　　　　　　E (D)　　　D (C)

*Gtr. 4

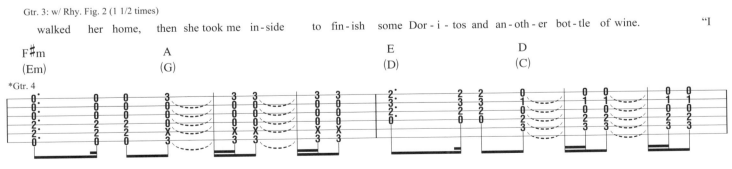

*Kybds. arr. for gtr.

swear I'm gon-na put you in a song that I write a-bout a Gal-way girl and a per-fect night." She

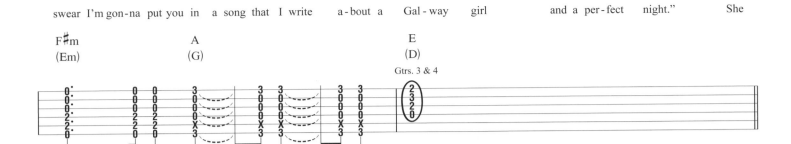

Pre-Chorus

Gtrs. 3 & 4 tacet

played the fid-dle in an I - rish band, but she fell in love with an Eng - lish - man. Kissed

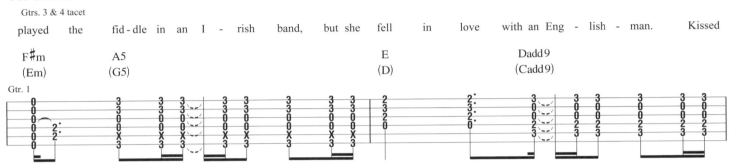

her on the neck and then I took her by the hand, said, "Ba - by, I just want to dance." My pret-ty lit-tle

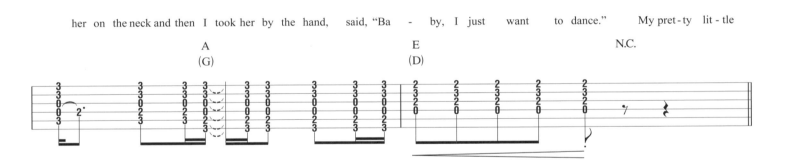

Chorus

Gtr. 1: w/ Rhy. Fig. 1 (4 times)
Gtr. 2: w/ Riff A (1st 3 meas.)

Dadd9	A5	E	F#m7
(Cadd9)	(G5)	(D)	(Em7)

Gal - way girl. My, my, my, my, my, my, my

Gtr. 2: w/ Fill 3

Dadd9	A5	E	F#m7
(Cadd9)	(G5)	(D)	(Em7)

Gal - way girl. My, my, my, my, my, my, my

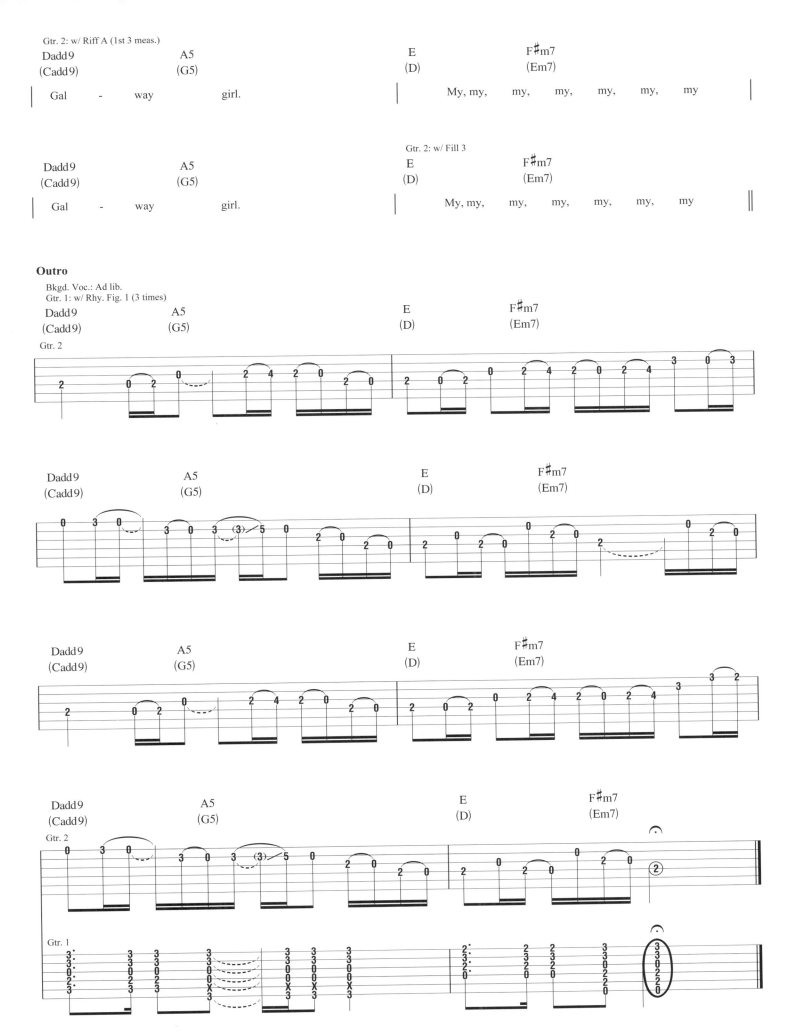

Happier

Words and Music by Ed Sheeran, Benjamin Levin and Ryan Tedder

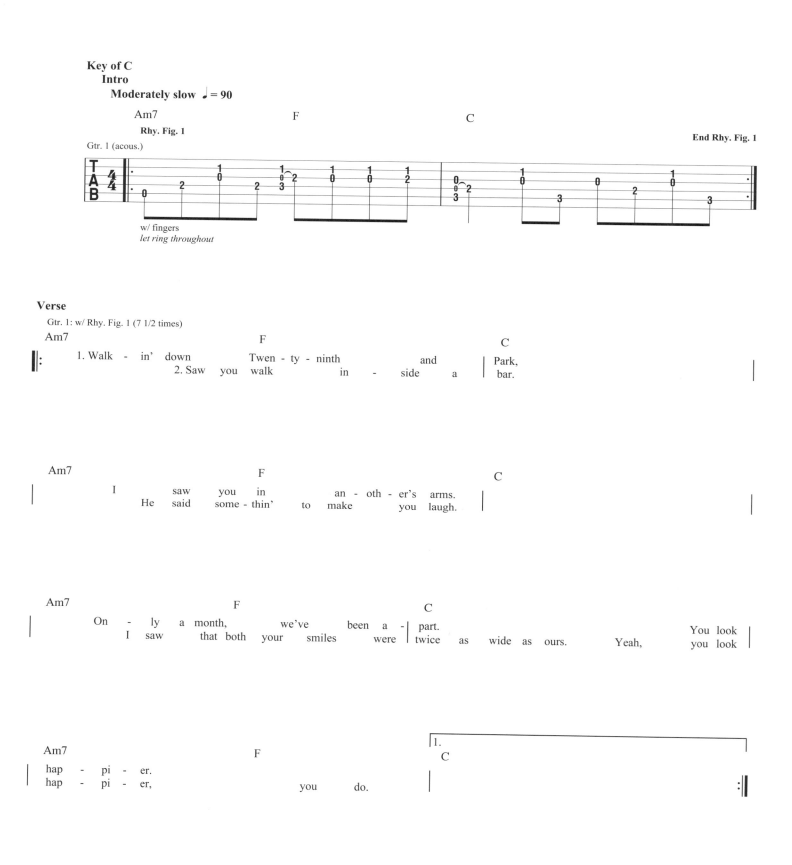

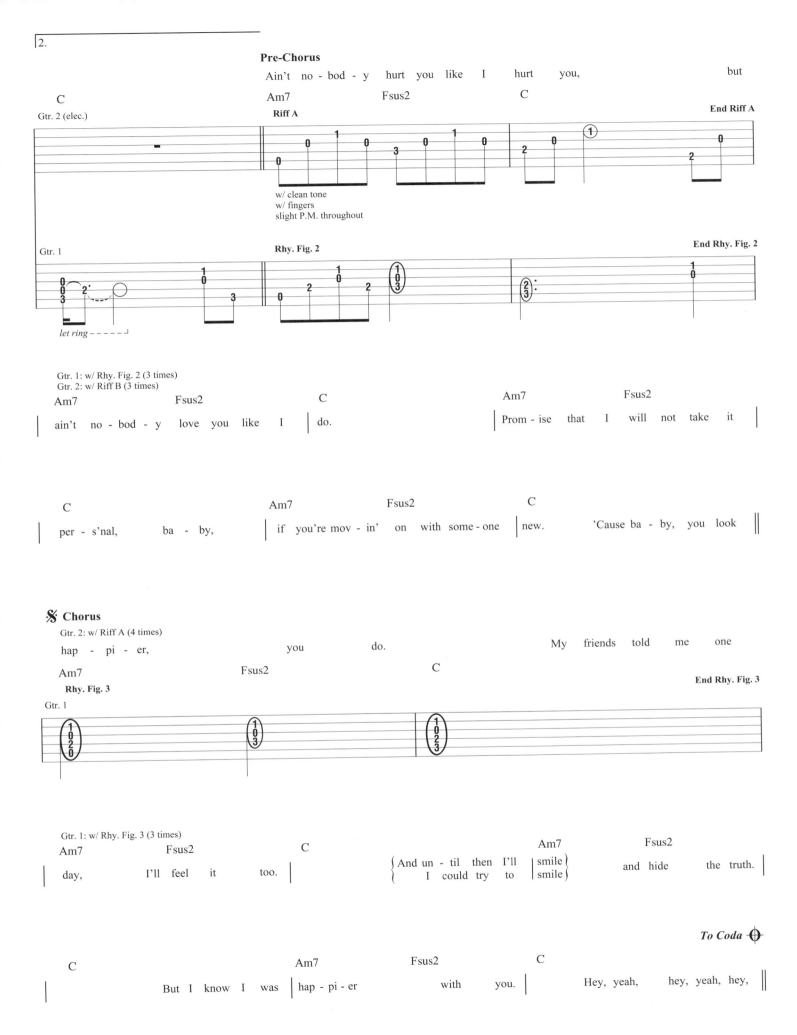

Verse

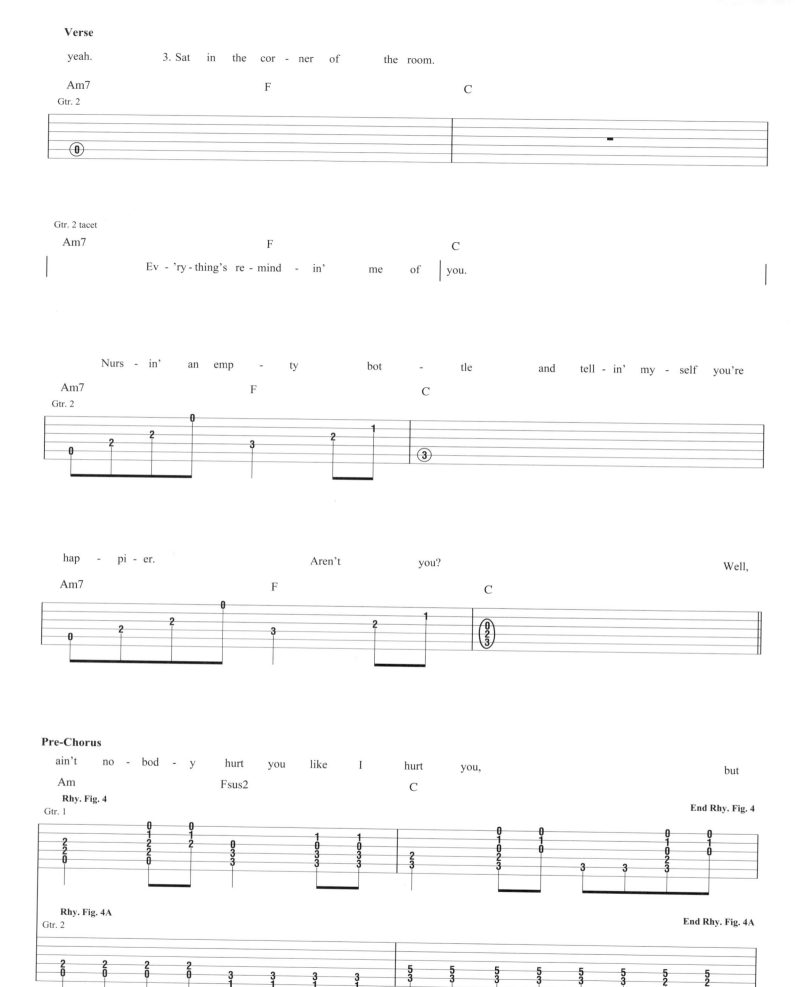

yeah.　　3. Sat　in　the　cor - ner　of　　the　room.

Am7　　　　　　　　　　F　　　　　　　　　C

Gtr. 2 tacet

Am7　　　　　　　　　　F　　　　　　　　　C

Ev - 'ry - thing's　re - mind - in'　　me　of　│you.

Nurs - in'　an　emp - ty　bot - tle　　and　tell - in'　my - self　you're

Am7　　　　　　　　　　F　　　　　　　　　C

Gtr. 2

hap - pi - er.　　　Aren't　　you?　　　　　　　　　Well,

Am7　　　　　　　　　　F　　　　　　　　　C

Pre-Chorus

ain't　no - bod - y　hurt　you　like　I　hurt　you,　　　　　but

Am　　　　　Fsus2　　　　　　　C

Rhy. Fig. 4　　　　　　　　　　　　　　　　　　End Rhy. Fig. 4

Gtr. 1

Rhy. Fig. 4A　　　　　　　　　　　　　　　　　End Rhy. Fig. 4A

Gtr. 2

P.M. - ┘

40

Gtrs. 1 & 2: w/ Rhy. Figs. 4 & 4A (2 times)

Am   Fsus2   C

ain't   no - bod - y   need   you   like   I | do.

Am   Fsus2   C

I   know   that   there's   oth - ers   that   de - | serve   you,   but   my

D.S. al Coda

dar - lin',   I   am   still   in   love   with   you.   But   I   guess   you   look

Am   Fsus2   C

Gtr. 1

Gtr. 2

P.M. -

⊕ Coda

Interlude

yeah.   Hey,   yeah,   hey,   yeah,   hey,

Am   Fsus2   C

Rhy. Fig. 5   **End Rhy. Fig. 5**

Gtr. 1

Gtr. 1: w/ Rhy. Fig. 5 (3 times)

Am   Fsus2   C

| yeah.   Hey,   yeah,   hey,   yeah,   hey, |

Am   Fsus2   C

| yeah.   Hey,   yeah,   hey,   yeah,   hey, |

Outro

hap - pi - er,   you   do.   I knew one day you'd

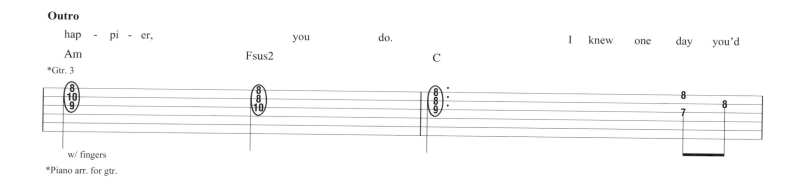

fall   for some - one new.   But if he breaks your

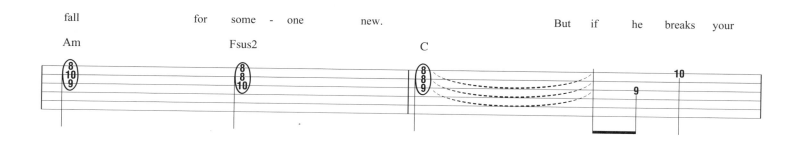

heart   like love - ers do,   just know that I'll be

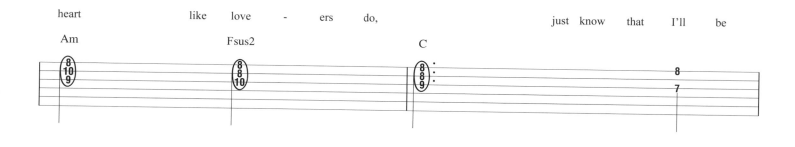

wait - in' here   for you.

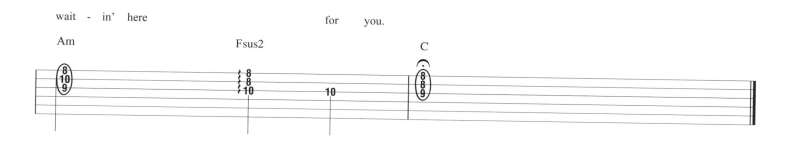

New Man

Words and Music by Ed Sheeran, Benjamin Levin, Jessie Ware and Ammar Malik

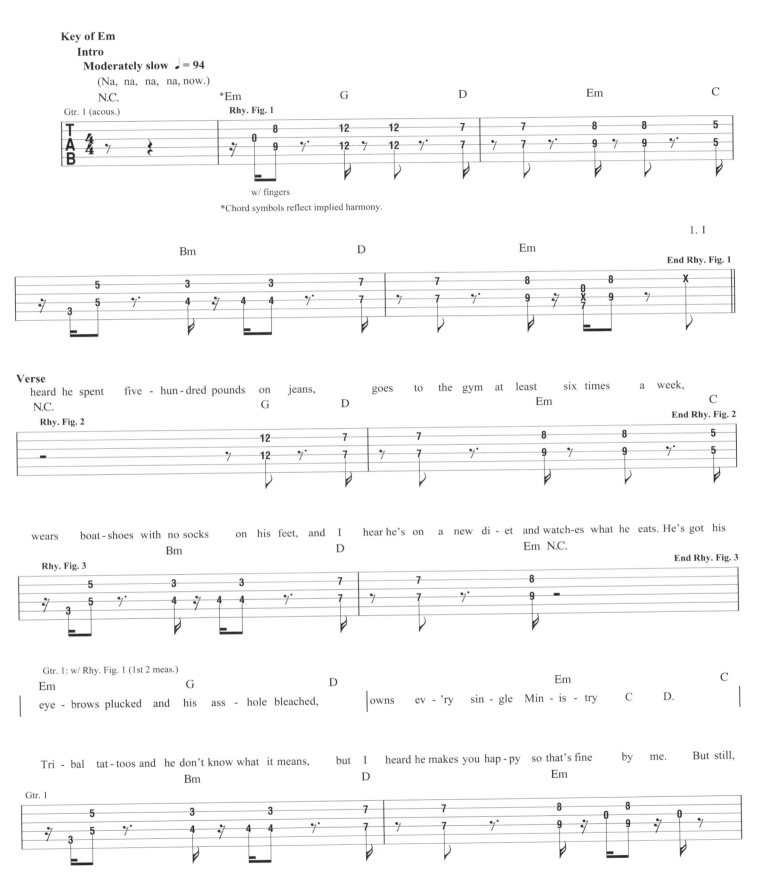

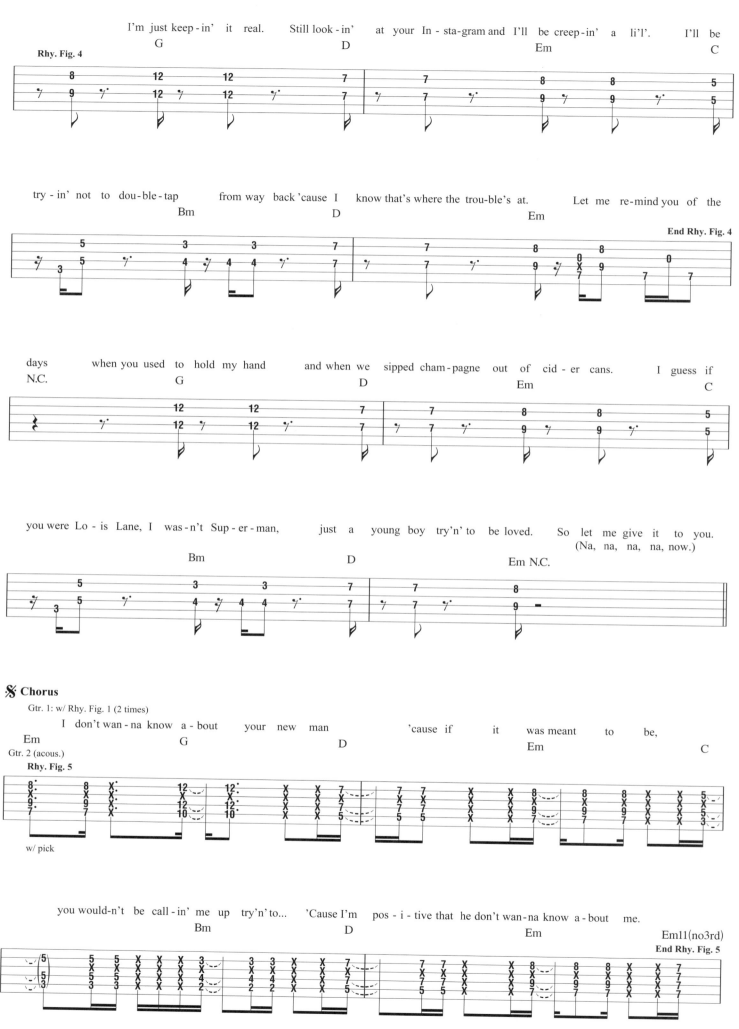

that   I   would   tell   you 'cause   you   ought-a   know.   You're   still   a   young   girl   try'n' to   be   loved,   so   let   me   give   it   to   you.
(Na,   na,   na,   na,   now.)

Bm   N.C.

Gtr. 1

Coda 1

pos - i - tive   that   he   don't   wan - na   know   a - bout   me.   Ba -

Em

Gtr. 2

Bridge

Gtr. 1: w/ Rhy. Fig. 1 (1 1/2 times)
Gtr. 2 tacet

Em   G   D   Em   C

by,   I'm   not   try'n'   to   ru - in   your |week,   but   you   act   so   dif - 'rent - |

Bm   D   Em   G   D

ly   when   you're   with   him.   I |know   you're   lone - ly. |Please   re - mem - ber   you're   still

Gtr. 1: w/ Rhy. Fig. 3

Em   C   Bm   D   Em N.C.

free   to   make   the   choice   and |leave.   Don't   call   me   up,   you |need   to   show   me.
(Na,   na,   na,   na,   now.)

Coda 2

pos - i - tive   that   he   don't   wan - na   know   a - bout   me.
(Na,   na,   na,   na,   now.)

Em   N.C.

Gtr. 2

Outro

Gtr. 2 tacet

Pos - i - tive   that   he   don't   wan - na   know   a - bout,   pos - i - tive   that   he   don't   wa,   wan - na   know   a - bout.

Em   G   D   Em   C

Gtr. 1

I   don't   wan - na   know   a - ba - ba -   bout   your   new   man.
(Na,   na,   na,   na,   now.)

Bm   D   Em N.C.

Hearts Don't Break Around Here

Words and Music by Ed Sheeran and Johnny McDaid

Capo VII

Key of G (Capo Key of C)
Verse
Moderately slow ♩ = 70

1. She is the sweet - est thing that I know.

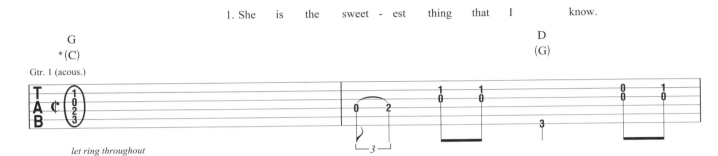

*Symbols in parentheses represent chord names respective to capoed guitar.
Symbols above reflect actual sounding chords.

Should see the way she holds me when the lights go low. Shakes my

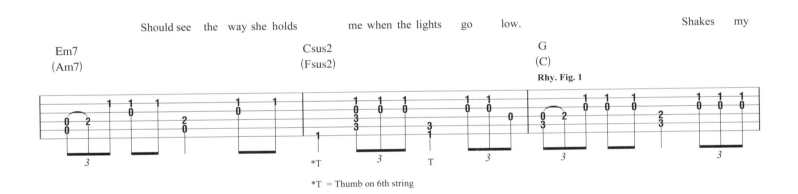

*T = Thumb on 6th string

soul like a pot - hole ev - 'ry time.

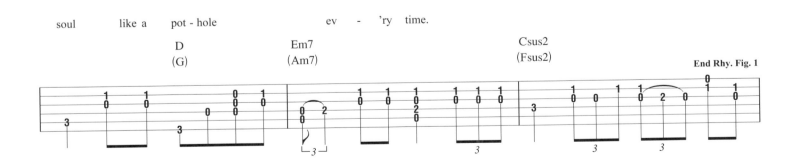

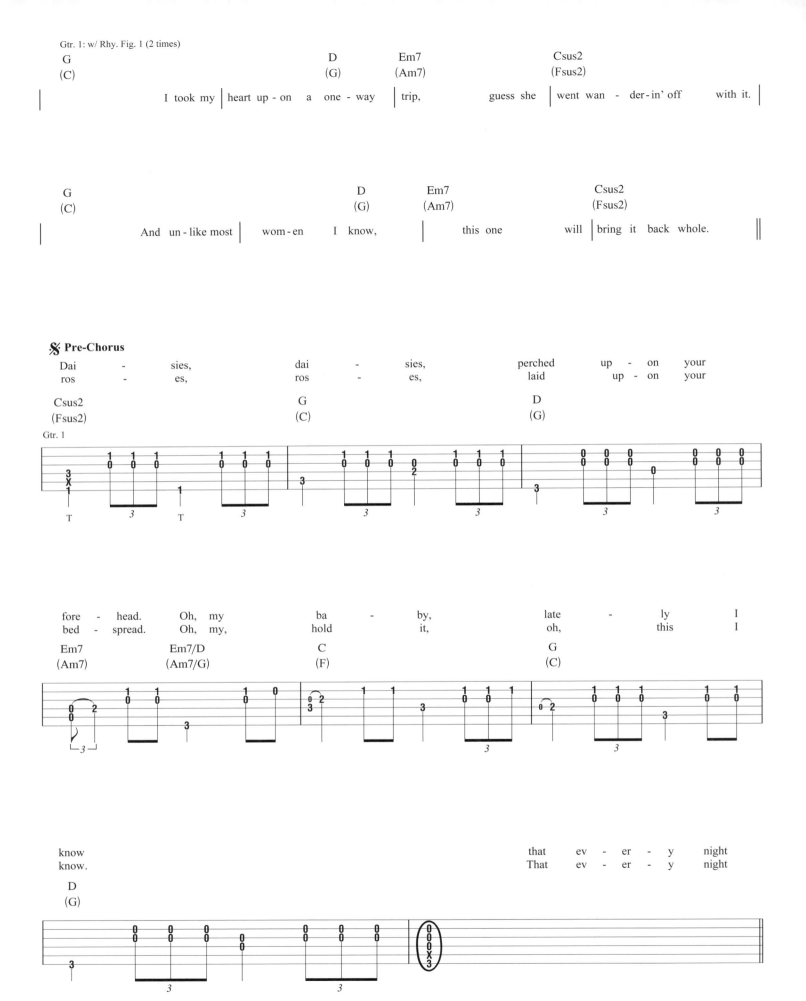

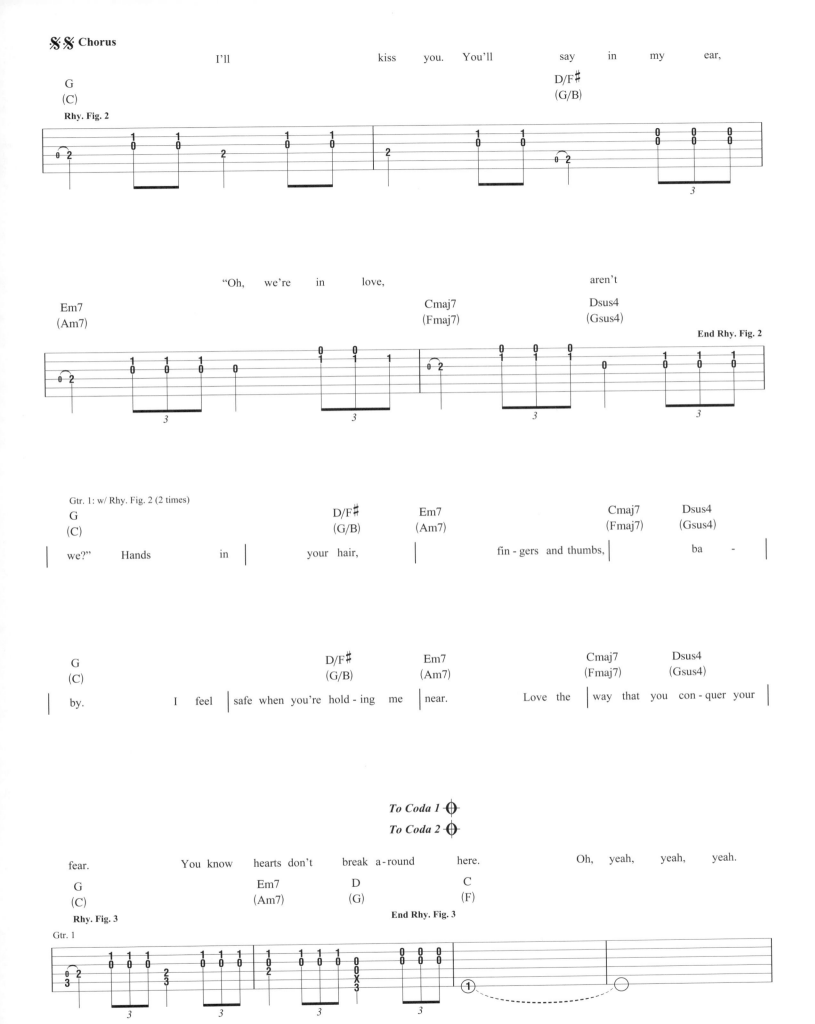

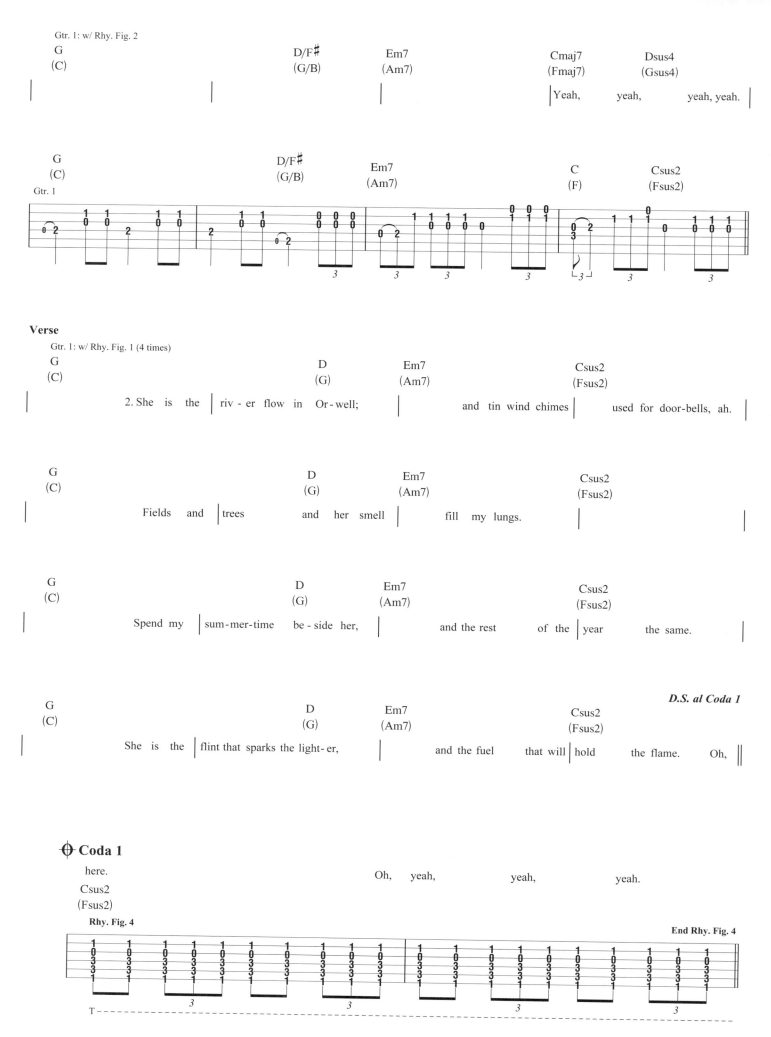

Gtr. 1: w/ Rhy. Fig. 2

| G | D/F# | Em7 | Cmaj7 | Dsus4 |
| (C) | (G/B) | (Am7) | (Fmaj7) | (Gsus4) |

Yeah,   yeah,   yeah, yeah.

| G | D/F# | Em7 | C | Csus2 |
| (C) | (G/B) | (Am7) | (F) | (Fsus2) |

Gtr. 1

Verse

Gtr. 1: w/ Rhy. Fig. 1 (4 times)

| G | D | Em7 | Csus2 |
| (C) | (G) | (Am7) | (Fsus2) |

2. She is the | riv - er flow in Or - well; | and tin wind chimes | used for door-bells, ah.

| G | D | Em7 | Csus2 |
| (C) | (G) | (Am7) | (Fsus2) |

Fields   and | trees   and her smell | fill my lungs.

| G | D | Em7 | Csus2 |
| (C) | (G) | (Am7) | (Fsus2) |

Spend my | sum-mer-time be - side her, | and the rest   of the | year   the same.

D.S. al Coda 1

| G | D | Em7 | Csus2 |
| (C) | (G) | (Am7) | (Fsus2) |

She is the | flint that sparks the light- er, | and the fuel   that will | hold   the flame.   Oh,

⊕ Coda 1

here.

Oh,   yeah,   yeah,   yeah.

Csus2
(Fsus2)

Rhy. Fig. 4

End Rhy. Fig. 4

50

Bridge

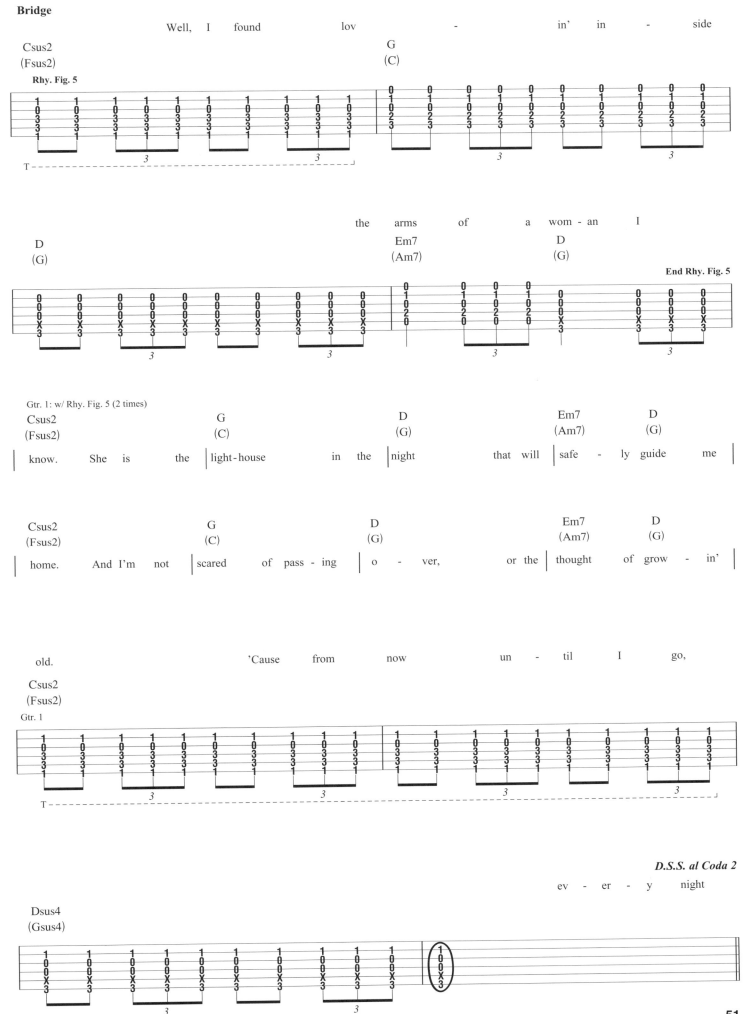

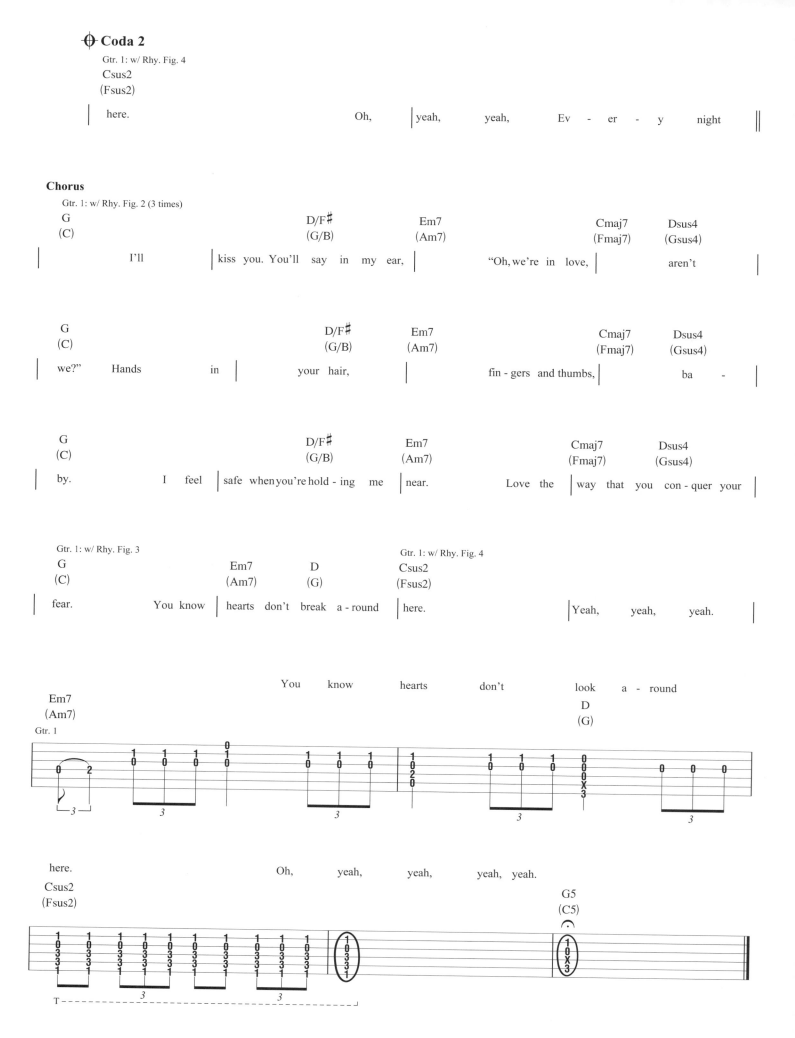

What Do I Know?

Words and Music by Ed Sheeran, Foy Vance and Johnny McDaid

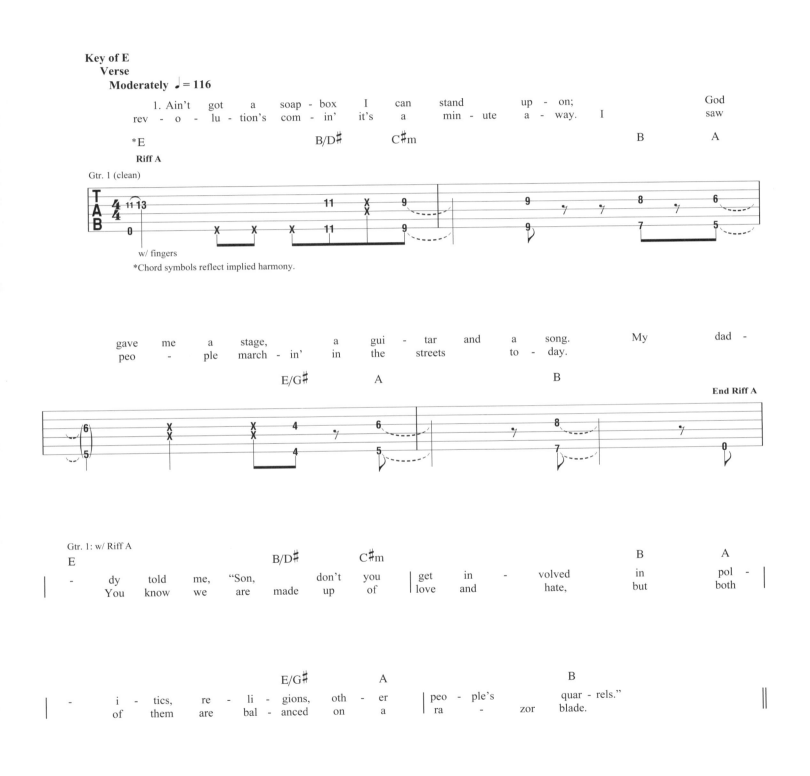

Key of E
Verse
Moderately ♩ = 116

1. Ain't got a soap-box I can stand up-on; God
rev-o-lu-tion's com-in' it's a min-ute a-way. I saw

*E   B/D#   C#m   B   A

gave me a stage, a gui-tar and a song. My dad-
peo-ple march-in' in the streets to-day.

E/G#   A   B   End Riff A

*Chord symbols reflect implied harmony.

Gtr. 1: w/ Riff A

E   B/D#   C#m   B   A
- dy told me, "Son, don't you get in-volved in pol-
  You know we are made up of love and both

E/G#   A   B
- i-tics, re-li-gions, oth-er peo-ple's quar-rels."
of them are bal-anced on a ra-zor blade.

Pre-Chorus

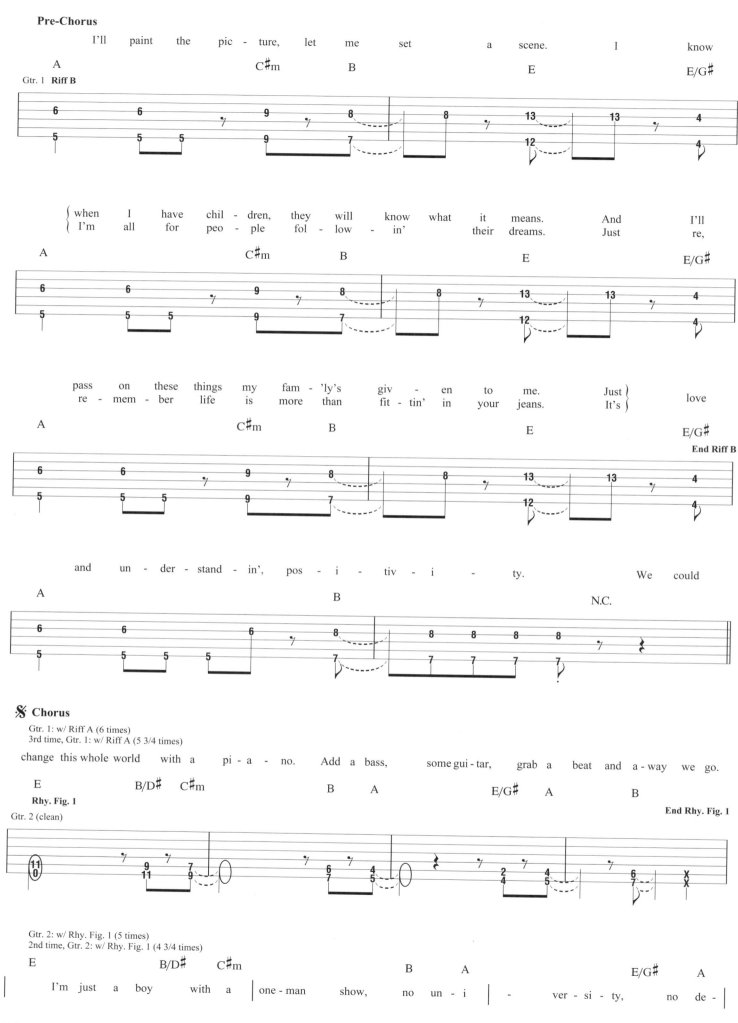

𝄋 Chorus

Gtr. 1: w/ Riff A (6 times)
3rd time, Gtr. 1: w/ Riff A (5 3/4 times)

Gtr. 2: w/ Rhy. Fig. 1 (5 times)
2nd time, Gtr. 2: w/ Rhy. Fig. 1 (4 3/4 times)

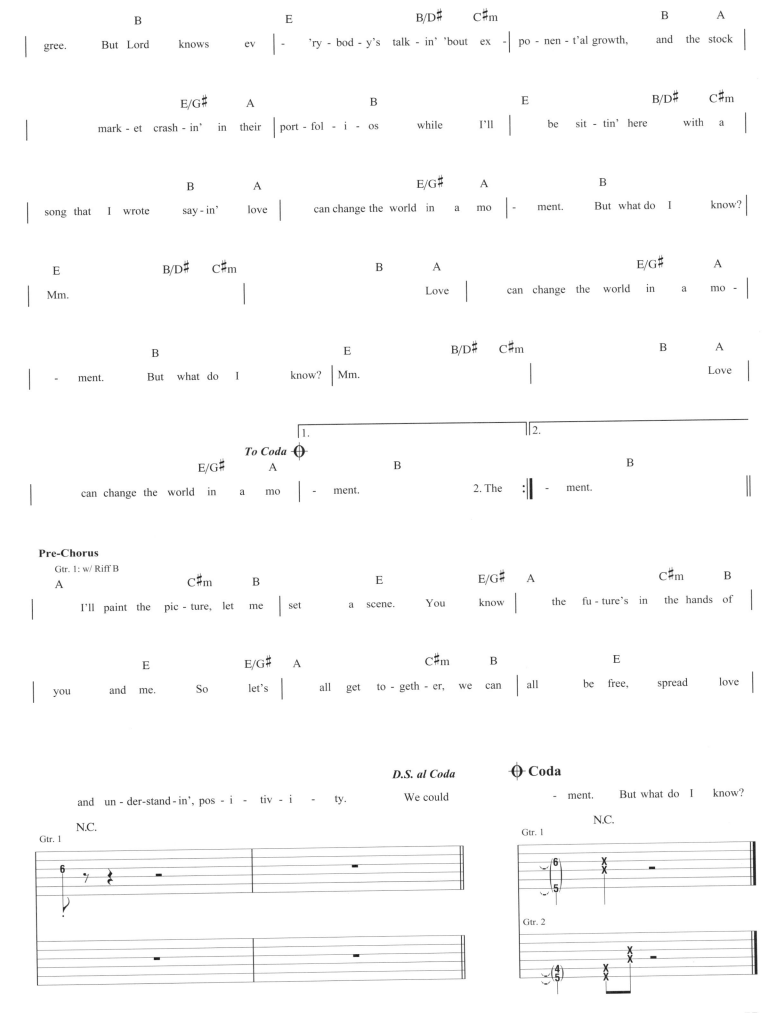

B			E		B/D♯	C♯m			B	A

gree. But Lord knows ev - 'ry - bod - y's talk - in' 'bout ex - po - nen - t'al growth, and the stock

	E/G♯	A		B		E		B/D♯	C♯m

mark - et crash - in' in their port - fol - i - os while I'll be sit - tin' here with a

B	A		E/G♯	A		B	

song that I wrote say - in' love can change the world in a mo - ment. But what do I know?

E	B/D♯	C♯m		B	A		E/G♯	A

Mm. Love can change the world in a mo -

B		E	B/D♯	C♯m		B	A

- ment. But what do I know? Mm. Love

1.

To Coda ⊕

E/G♯	A		B			B

can change the world in a mo - ment. 2. The 𝄆 - ment.

2.

Pre-Chorus

Gtr. 1: w/ Riff B

A		C♯m	B		E		E/G♯	A		C♯m	B

I'll paint the pic - ture, let me set a scene. You know the fu - ture's in the hands of

	E	E/G♯	A		C♯m	B		E

you and me. So let's all get to - geth - er, we can all be free, spread love

D.S. al Coda   ⊕ **Coda**

and un - der - stand - in', pos - i - tiv - i - ty. We could   - ment. But what do I know?

How Would You Feel
(Paean)

Words and Music by Ed Sheeran

Gtr. 1 Capo II

Key of A (Capo Key of G)
Intro
Moderately slow ♩ = 70

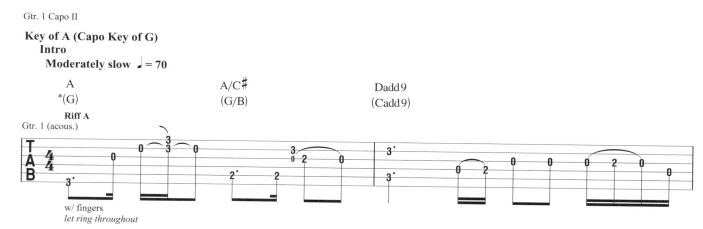

*Symbols in parentheses represent chord names respective to capoed guitar.
Symbols above reflect actual sounding chords. Capoed fret is "0" in tab.

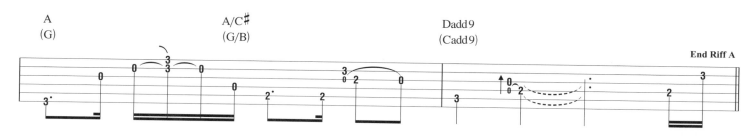

Verse

1. You are the one,   girl,   and you know that   it's   true.
2. In the sum - mer,   as   the   li - lacs   bloom,

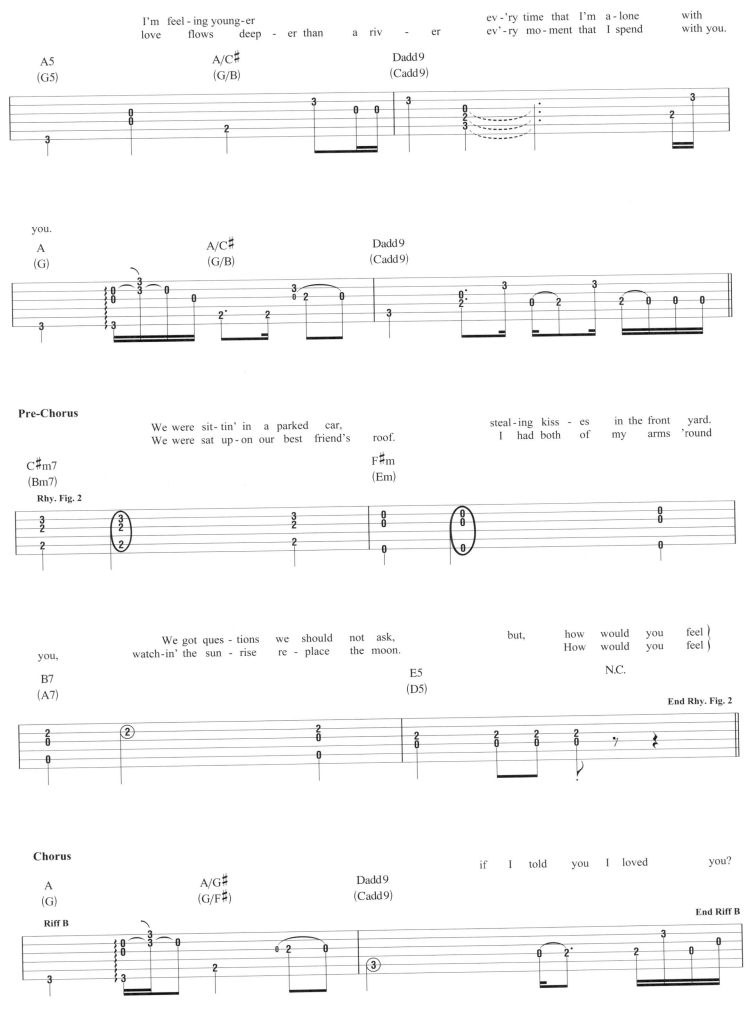

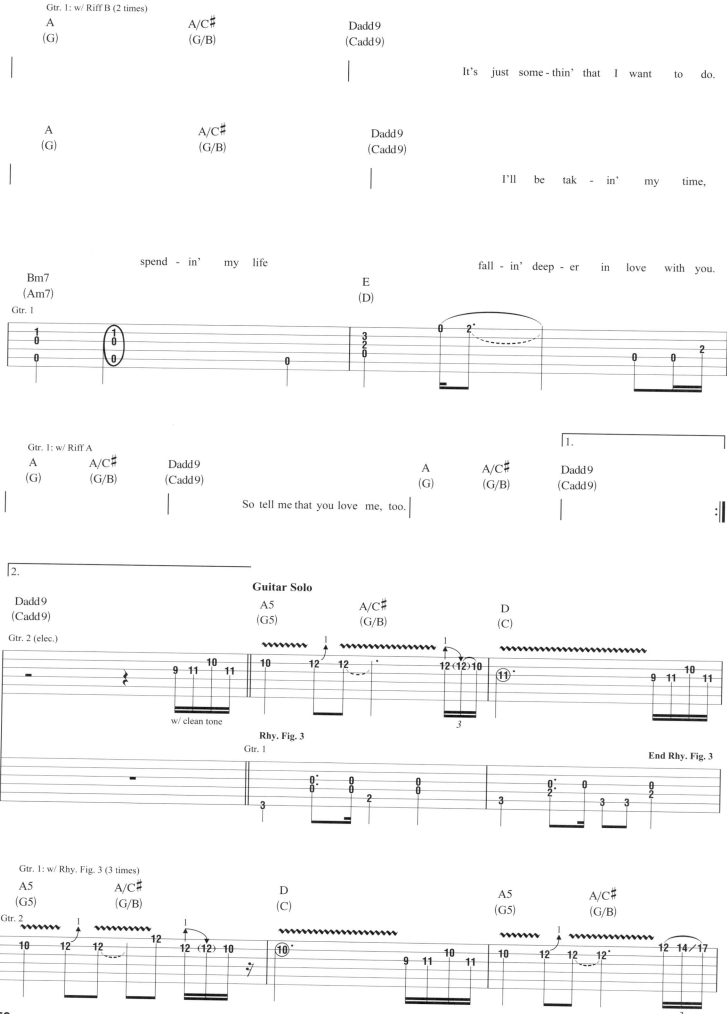

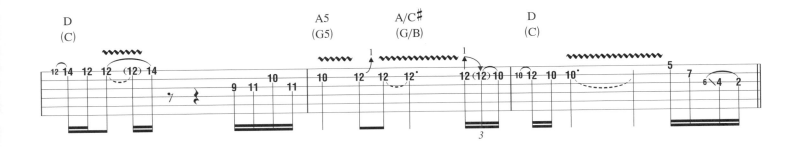

Pre-Chorus

Gtr. 1: w/ Rhy. Fig. 2

Yeah, we were sit - tin' in a parked car, steal - ing kiss - es in the front yard.

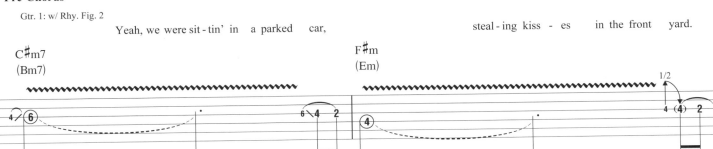

We got ques - tions we should not ask. How would you feel

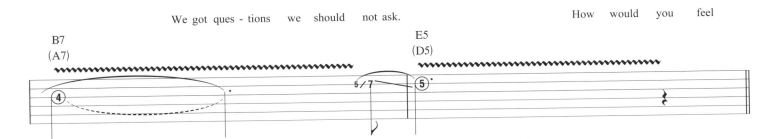

Chorus

if I told you I loved you?

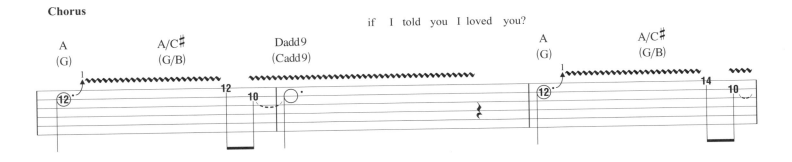

It's just some - thin' that I want to do. I'll be tak - in' my time,

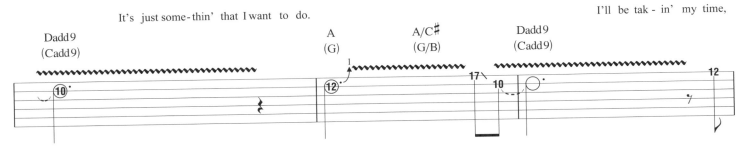

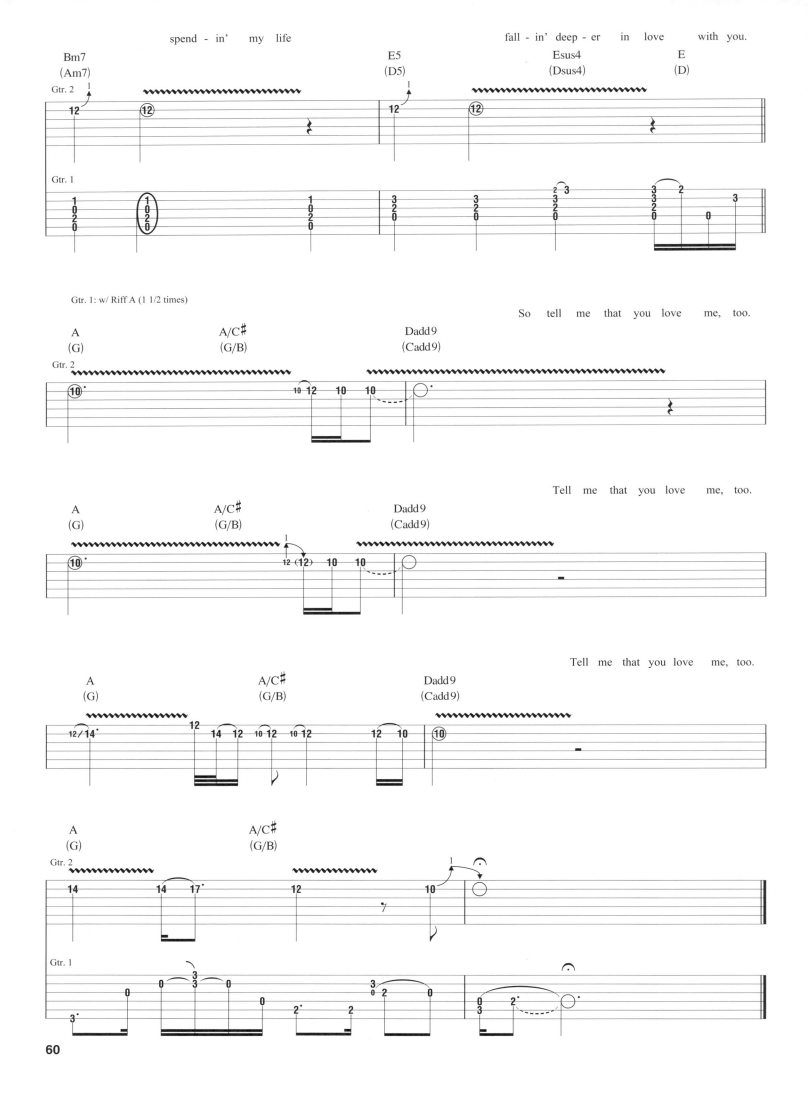

Supermarket Flowers

Words and Music by Ed Sheeran, Benjamin Levin and Johnny McDaid

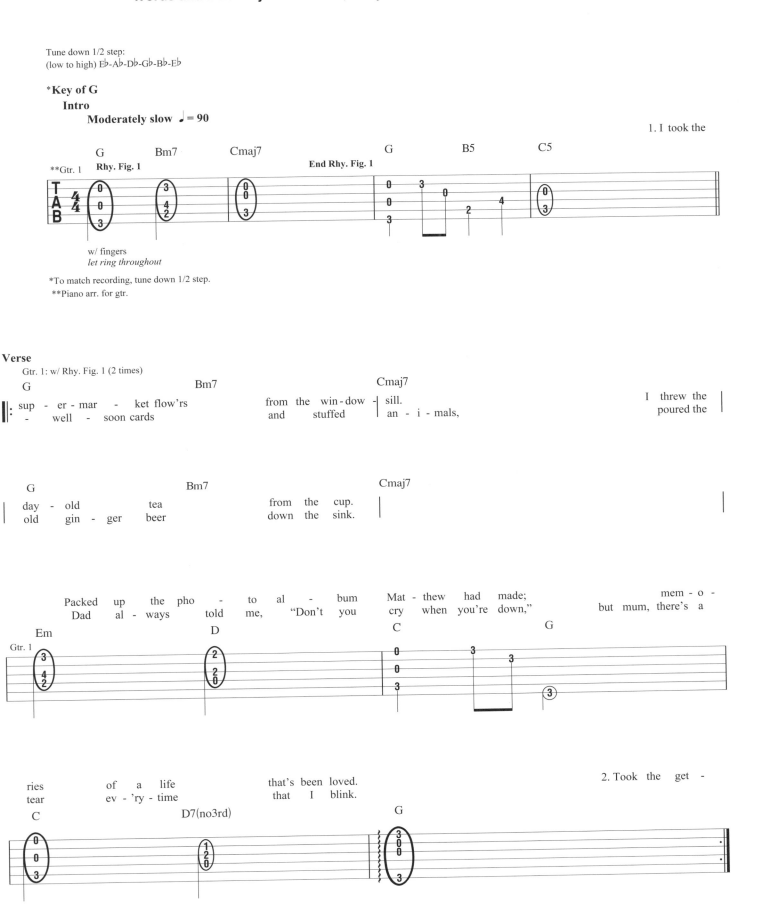

% Pre-Chorus

Oh, I'm in piec - es. It's tear - in' me up, but I know
And I hope that I see the world as you did, 'cause I know

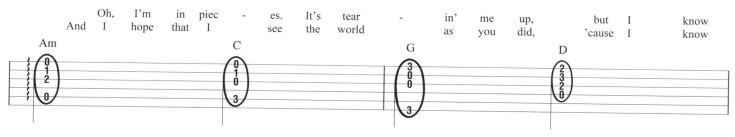

a heart that's broke is a heart that's been loved. } So I'll sing
a life with love is a life that's been lived. }

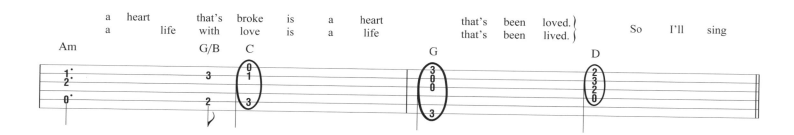

Chorus

Hal - le - lu - jah, you were an an - gel in the shape of my mum. When I fell down, you'd be there

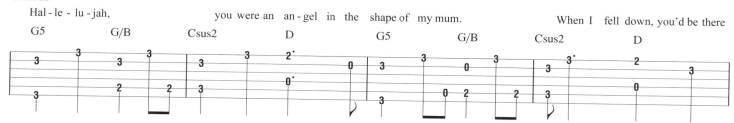

To Coda

hold-in' me up. Spread your wings as you go, and when God takes you back, He'll say "Hal - le - lu -jah, you're home."

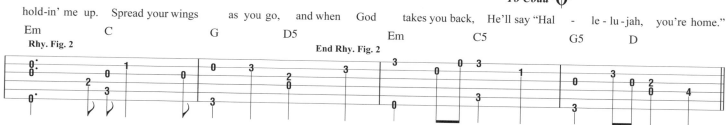

Interlude

3. I fluffed the pil-

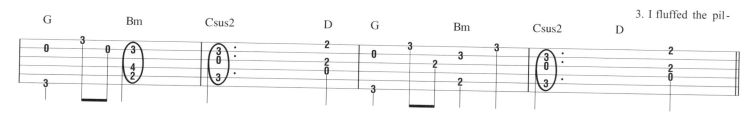

Verse

lows, made the bed, stacked the chairs up, fold - ed your night - gowns neat - ly in a case.

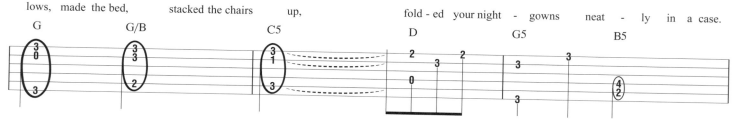

62

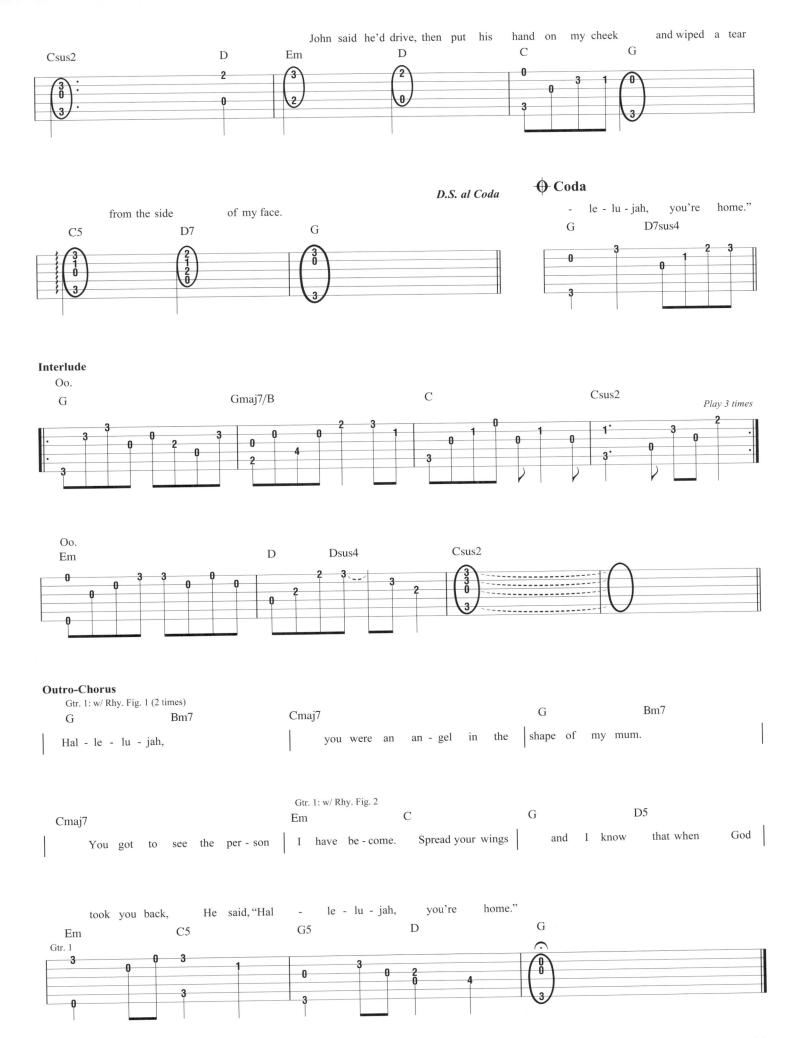

Barcelona

Words and Music by Ed Sheeran, Benjamin Levin, Foy Vance, Amy Wadge and Johnny McDaid

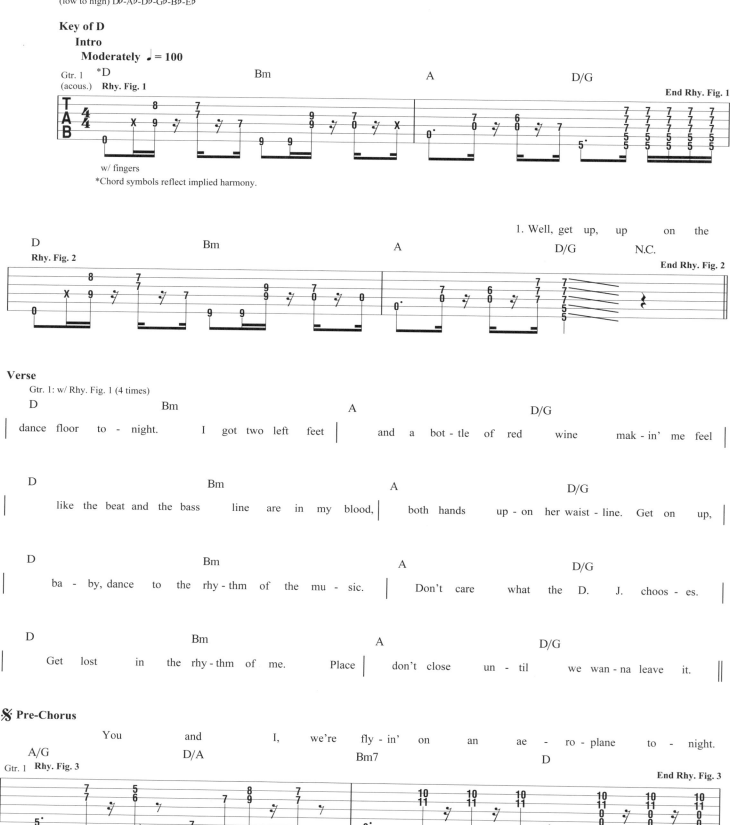

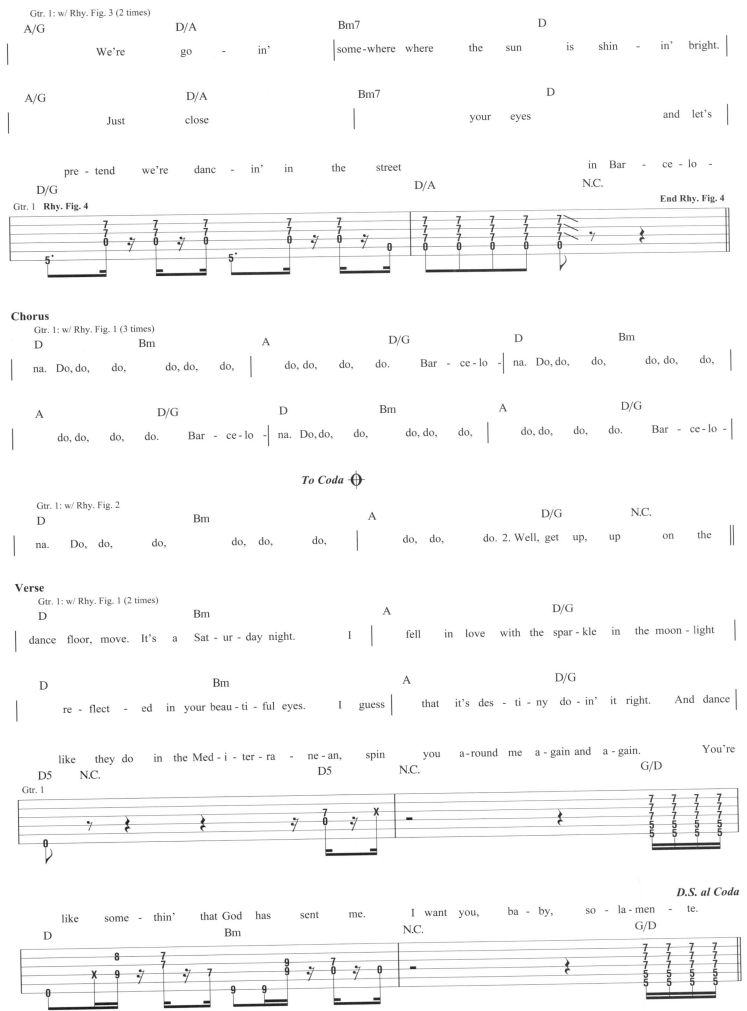

⊕ Coda

Interlude

Gtr. 1: w/ Rhy. Fig. 3 (3 times)

| A | D/G | N.C. | A/G | D/A | Bm7 | D |

do, do, do, do. In Bar - ce - lo - ‖ na   Bar - ce - lo -|

| A/G | D/A | Bm7 | D | A/G | D/A |

na.   Oh, Bar - ce - lo - | na.

Gtr. 1: w/ Rhy. Fig. 4

| Bm7 | D | D/G | | D/A | N.C. |

So let's | pre - tend we're danc - in' in the street | in Bar - ce - lo - ‖

Outro-Chorus

Gtr. 1: w/ Rhy. Fig. 1 (8 times)

| D | Bm | A | D/G |

na. Los Ram - blas,   I'll meet   you. We'll | dance a - round   La Sa - gra - da   Fa - mil - ia. |

| D | Bm | A | D/G |

Drink - in'   San - gri - a, | mi ni - ña, te a - mo mi ca - ri - ño. |

| D | Bm | A | D/G |

Ma - ma - ci - ta,   ri - ca, | si tú,   te a - do - ro se - ño - ri - ta. |

| D | Bm | A | D/G |

Los o - tros,   vi - v'la vi - da. | Come on, let's be free   in Bar - ce - lo - |

| D | Bm | A | D/G |

na. Los Ram - blas,   I'll meet   you. | Come on and dance with me   in Bar - ce - lo - |

| D | Bm | A | D/G |

na.   Drink - in'   San - gri - a, | I just want to be   in Bar - ce - lo - |

| D | Bm | A | D/G |

na. Ma - ma - ci - ta,   ri - ca. | Feel that   sum - mer breeze in Bar - ce - lo - |

| D | Bm | A | D/G | N.C. |

na. Los o - tros,   vi - v'la vi - da. | Si - em - pre vi - da Bar - ce - lo - | na.

Bibia Be Ye Ye

Words and Music by Ed Sheeran, Benjamin Levin, Nana Richard Abiona, Joseph Addison and Stephen Woode

Gtr. 2: Capo V

Key of G (Capo Key of D)

Intro

Moderately fast ♩ = 127

G5   *(D)
Am7 (Em7)
C5 (G5)
D (A)

Gtr. 3 (clean)   Riff A   End Riff A

slight P.M. throughout

Gtr. 2 (clean)   Rhy. Fig. 1A   End Rhy. Fig. 1A

Gtr. 1 (clean)   Rhy. Fig. 1   End Rhy. Fig. 1

*Symbols in parentheses represent chord names respective to capoed gtr.
Symbols above reflect actual sounding chords. Capoed fret is "0" in tab.

Gtrs. 1 & 2: w/ Rhy. Figs. 1 & 1A (3 times)
Gtr. 3: w/ Riff A

G5 (D)
Am7 (Em7)
C5 (G5)
D (A)

Bi - bi - a   be   ye   ye.

G5 (D)
Am7 (Em7)
C5 (G5)
D (A)

Gtr. 3

G5 (D)
Am7 (Em7)
C5 (G5)
D (A)

Verse

*Gtrs. 1 & 2: w/ Rhy. Figs. 1 & 1A (4 times)
1st time, Gtr. 3 tacet
2nd time, Gtr. 3: w/ Fill 1 (4 times)

G5	Am7	C5	D
(D)	(Em7)	(G5)	(A)

1. I lost my shoes last night.   I don't know where I put my
3. I re-mem-ber less and less,   and most-ly things that I re-gret.

*Roll back tone controls

G5	Am7	C5	D
(D)	(Em7)	(G5)	(A)

keys.   In my phone are sev-'ral texts   and fell a-sleep be-neath an oak
       I was tired   from girls I've nev-er met.

G5	Am7	C5	D
(D)	(Em7)	(G5)	(A)

tree.   I bet my moth-er's proud of me from each scar
And in the pock-et of my jeans are on-ly coins and brok-en dreams.

G5	Am7	C5	D
(D)	(Em7)	(G5)	(A)

up-on my knuck-le and each graze up-on my knee. 2. And all I
My heart is break-in' at the seams and I'm com-in' a-part now.

Verse

**Gtrs. 1 & 2: w/ Rhy. Figs. 1 & 1A (4 times)
2nd time, Gtr. 3: w/ Fill 1

know   is I got a cab   and then threw up up-on his car
4. Now things are look-in' up; I'll find my shoes right next to the oak

G5	Am7	C5	D
(D)	(Em7)	(G5)	(A)

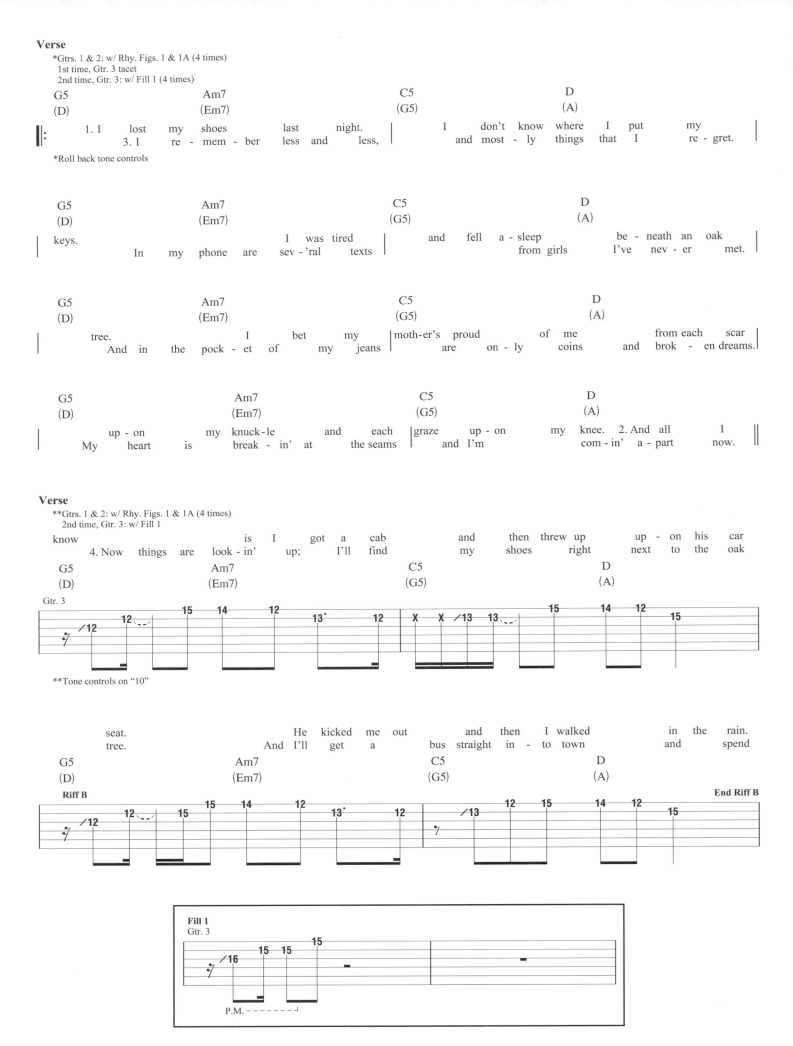

**Tone controls on "10"

seat.   He kicked me out and then I walked in the rain.
tree.   And I'll get a bus straight in-to town and spend

G5	Am7	C5	D
(D)	(Em7)	(G5)	(A)

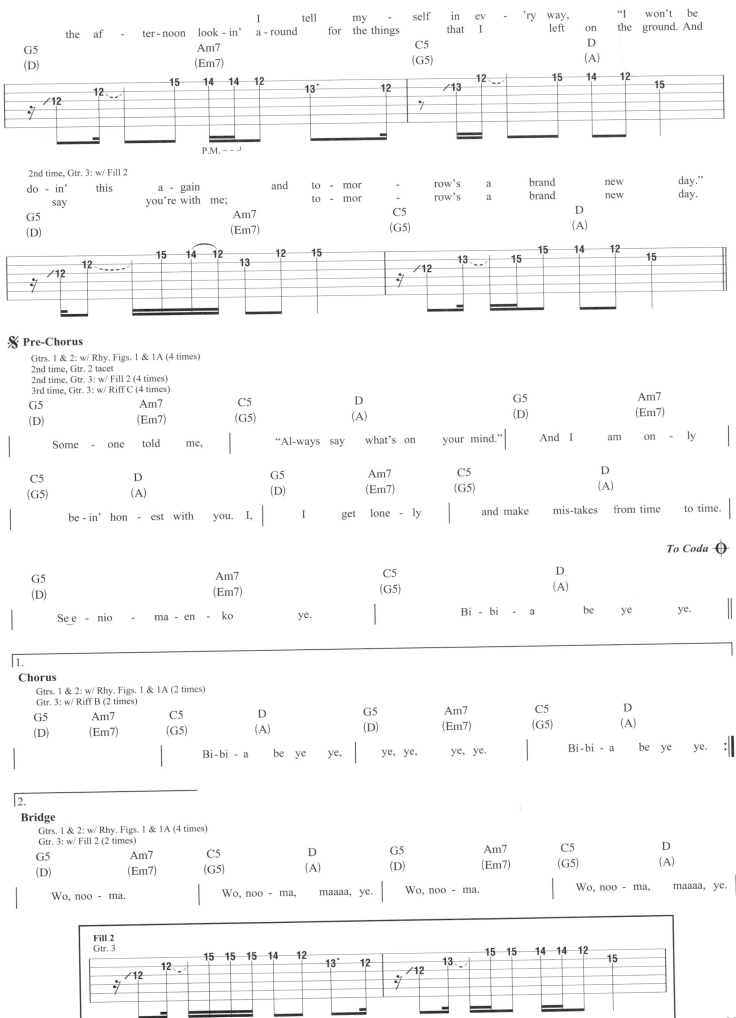

the af - ter-noon look - in' a - round for the things
I tell my - self in ev - 'ry way, "I won't be
that I left on the ground. And

G5
(D)
Am7
(Em7)
C5
(G5)
D
(A)

2nd time, Gtr. 3: w/ Fill 2

do - in' this a - gain and to - mor - row's a brand new day."
say you're with me; to - mor - row's a brand new day.

G5
(D)
Am7
(Em7)
C5
(G5)
D
(A)

𝄋 Pre-Chorus

Gtrs. 1 & 2: w/ Rhy. Figs. 1 & 1A (4 times)
2nd time, Gtr. 2 tacet
2nd time, Gtr. 3: w/ Fill 2 (4 times)
3rd time, Gtr. 3: w/ Riff C (4 times)

G5   **Am7**   **C5**   **D**   **G5**   **Am7**
(D)   **(Em7)**   **(G5)**   **(A)**   **(D)**   **(Em7)**

Some - one told me, "Al-ways say what's on your mind." And I am on - ly

C5   **D**   **G5**   **Am7**   **C5**   **D**
(G5)   **(A)**   **(D)**   **(Em7)**   **(G5)**   **(A)**

be - in' hon - est with you. I, I get lone - ly and make mis-takes from time to time.

To Coda ⊕

G5   **Am7**   **C5**   **D**
(D)   **(Em7)**   **(G5)**   **(A)**

Se e - nio - ma - en - ko ye. Bi - bi - a be ye ye.

1.

Chorus

Gtrs. 1 & 2: w/ Rhy. Figs. 1 & 1A (2 times)
Gtr. 3: w/ Riff B (2 times)

G5   **Am7**   **C5**   **D**   **G5**   **Am7**   **C5**   **D**
(D)   **(Em7)**   **(G5)**   **(A)**   **(D)**   **(Em7)**   **(G5)**   **(A)**

Bi - bi - a be ye ye, ye, ye, ye, ye. Bi - bi - a be ye ye.

2.

Bridge

Gtrs. 1 & 2: w/ Rhy. Figs. 1 & 1A (4 times)
Gtr. 3: w/ Fill 2 (2 times)

G5   **Am7**   **C5**   **D**   **G5**   **Am7**   **C5**   **D**
(D)   **(Em7)**   **(G5)**   **(A)**   **(D)**   **(Em7)**   **(G5)**   **(A)**

Wo, noo - ma. Wo, noo - ma, maaaa, ye. Wo, noo - ma. Wo, noo - ma, maaaa, ye.

Fill 2
Gtr. 3

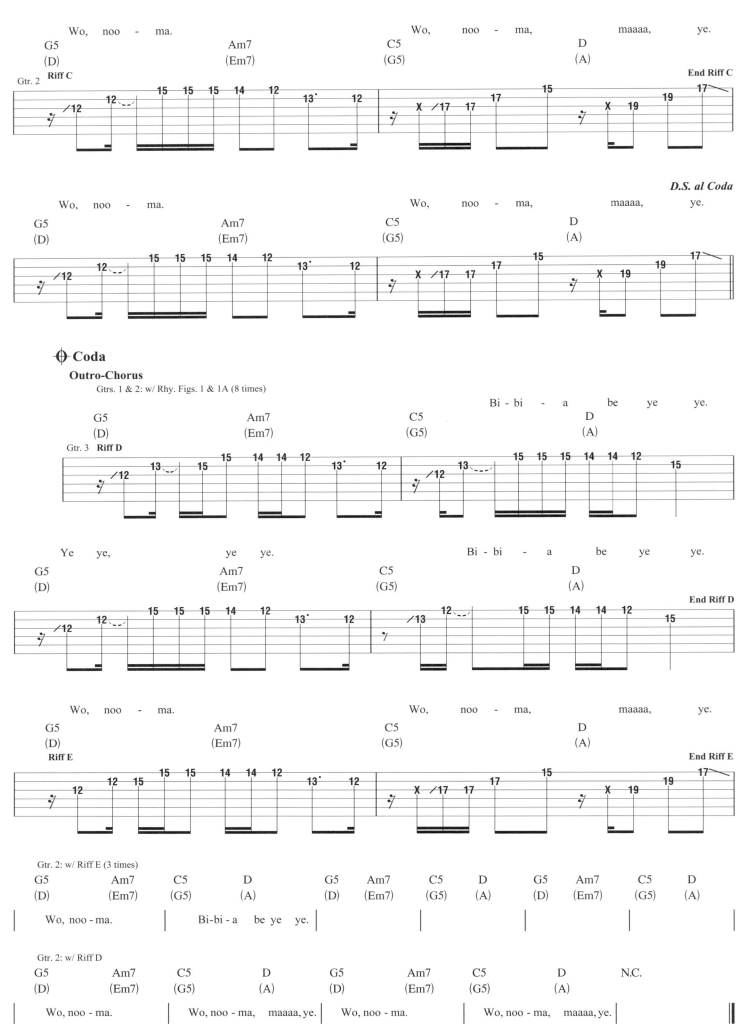

Nancy Mulligan

Words and Music by Ed Sheeran, Murray Cummings, Benjamin Levin, Foy Vance, Amy Wadge and Johnny McDaid

Key of G
Intro
Moderately ♩ = 102

(Hey!)

Gtr. 1 *Em
(acous.) Riff A

*Chord symbols reflect implied harmony.

(Hey!)

End Riff A

Verse

Gtr. 1: w/ Riff A

1. I was twen-ty-four years old when I met the wom-an I would call my own. Twen-ty-
Em7   Cadd9   D5/A   Em7

**Gtr. 2 (acous.)
Rhy. Fig. 1

**Doubled throughout

two grand kids, now grow-in' old in that house that your broth-er bought you.
Cadd9   G5   Cadd9   D5/A   Em7

End Rhy. Fig. 1

Gtr. 1: w/ Riff A (last 2 meas., 2 times)
Gtr. 2 tacet

Em

On the

Gtr. 2: w/ Rhy. Fig. 1
Em7   Cadd9   D5/A   Em7

sum-mer day when I pro-posed, I made that wed-ding ring from den-tist gold. And I

Gtr. 1: w/ Riff A (1st 2 meas.)
      Cadd9   G5   Cadd9   D5/A   Em7

asked her fath-er, but her dad-dy said, "No, you can't mar-ry my daugh-ter."

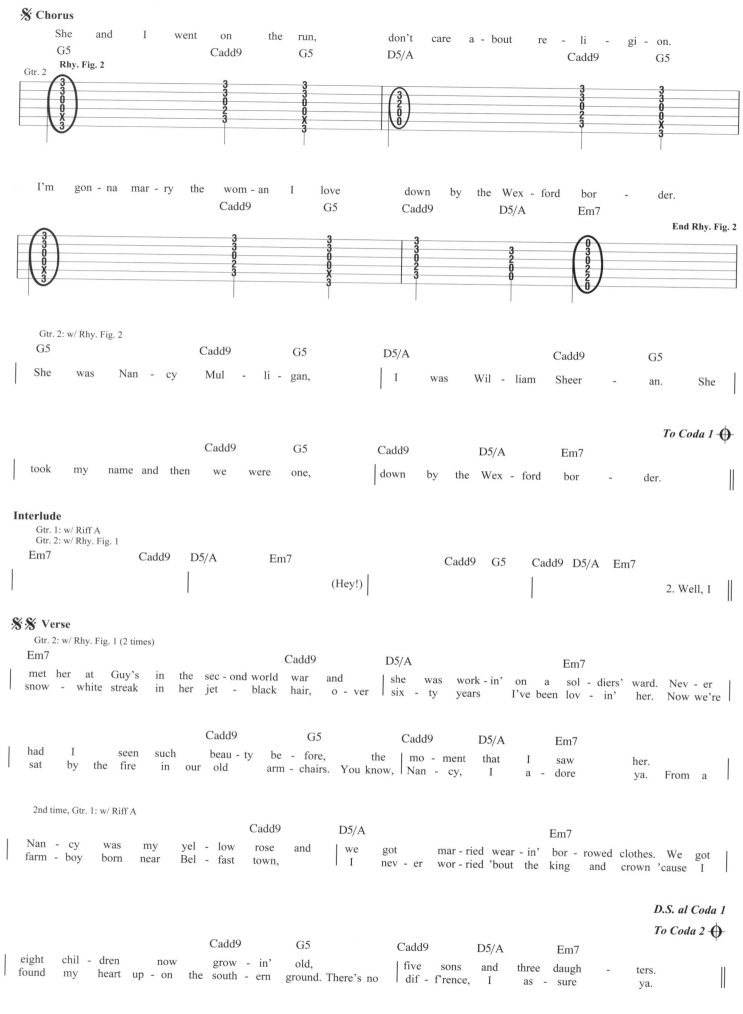

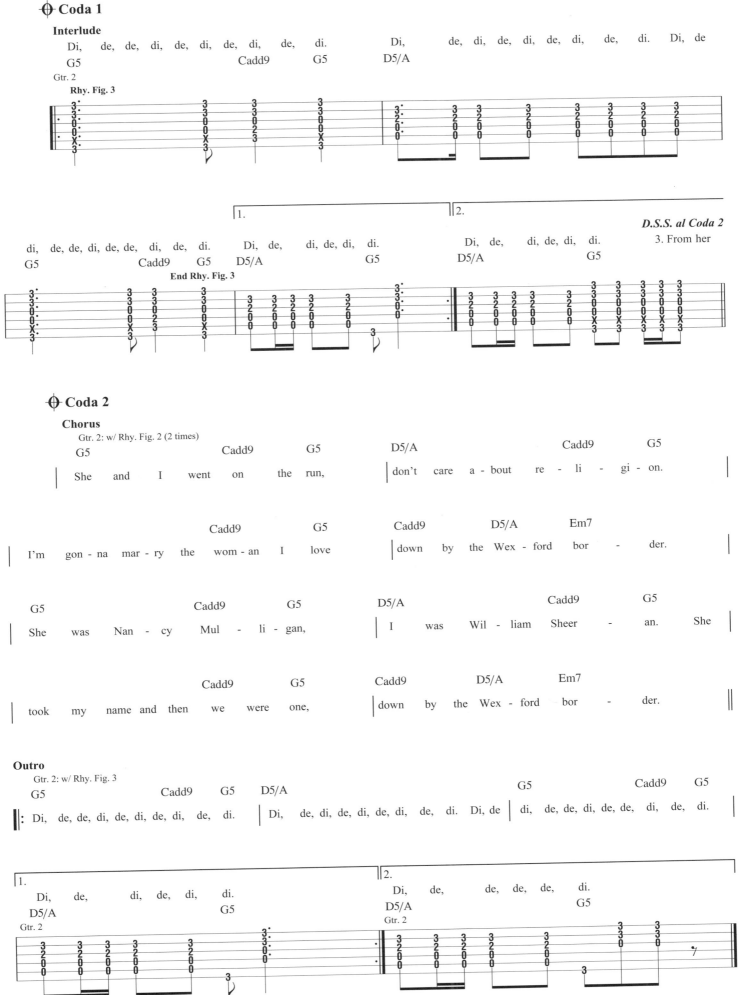

Save Myself

Words and Music by Ed Sheeran, Timothy Mckenzie and Amy Wadge

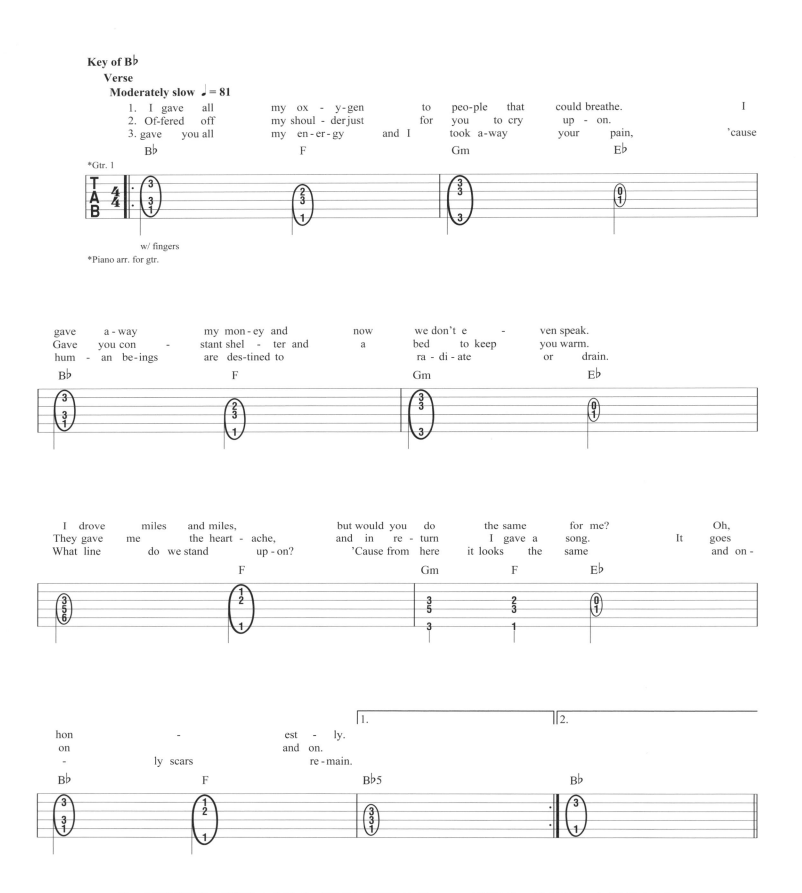

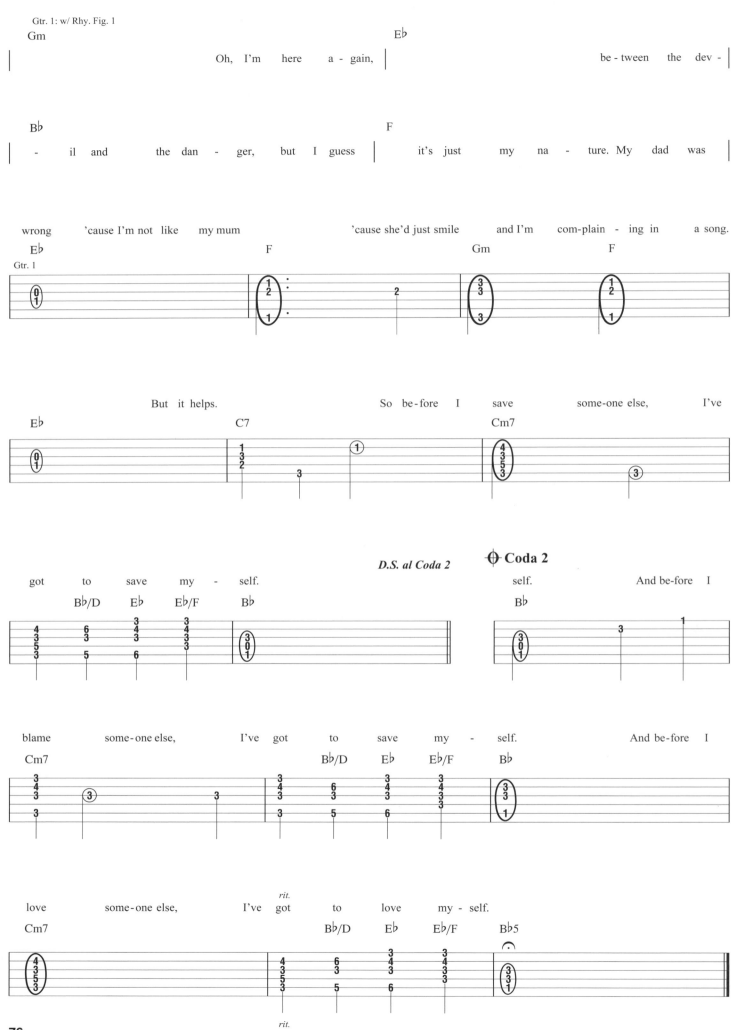

RHYTHM TAB LEGEND

Rhythm Tab is a form of notation that adds rhythmic values to the traditional tab staff.

TABLATURE graphically represents the guitar fingerboard. Each horizontal line represents a string, and each number represents a fret. Rhythmic values are shown using ovals, stems, and dots.

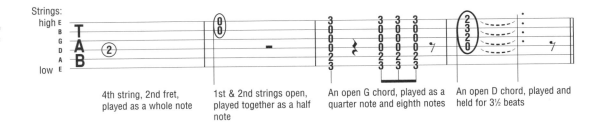

4th string, 2nd fret, played as a whole note

1st & 2nd strings open, played together as a half note

An open G chord, played as a quarter note and eighth notes

An open D chord, played and held for 3½ beats

Definitions for Special Guitar Notation

HALF-STEP BEND: Strike the note and bend up 1/2 step.

WHOLE-STEP BEND: Strike the note and bend up one step.

SLIGHT (MICROTONE) BEND: Strike the note and bend up 1/4 step.

BEND AND RELEASE: Strike the note and bend up as indicated, then release back to the original note. Only the first note is struck.

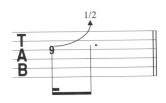
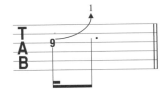
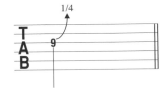
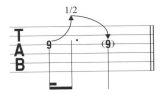

PRE-BEND: Bend the note as indicated, then strike it.

GRACE NOTE PRE-BEND AND RELEASE: Bend the note as indicated. Strike it and release the bend back to the original note.

UNISON BEND: Strike the two notes simultaneously and bend the lower note up to the pitch of the higher.

HOLD BEND: While sustaining bent note, strike note on different string.

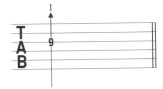
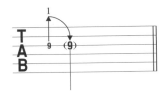
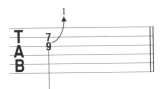
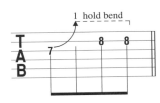

VIBRATO: The string is vibrated by rapidly bending and releasing the note with the fretting hand.

WIDE VIBRATO: The pitch is varied to a greater degree by vibrating with the fretting hand.

HAMMER-ON: Strike the first (lower) note with one finger, then sound the higher note (on the same string) with another finger by fretting it without picking.

PULL-OFF: Place both fingers on the notes to be sounded. Strike the first note and without picking, pull the finger off to sound the second (lower) note.

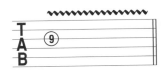
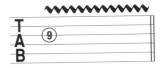

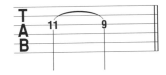
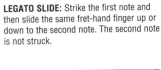

HAMMER FROM NOWHERE: Sound note(s) by hammering with fret hand finger only.

GRACE NOTE SLUR: Strike the note and immediately hammer-on (or pull-off) as indicated.

GRACE NOTE SLUR (CLUSTER): Strike the notes and immediately hammer-on (or pull-off) as indicated.

LEGATO SLIDE: Strike the first note and then slide the same fret-hand finger up or down to the second note. The second note is not struck.

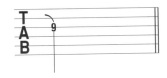

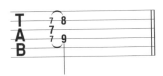
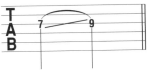

SHIFT SLIDE: Same as legato slide, except the second note is struck.

GRACE NOTE SLIDE: Quickly slide into the note from below or above.

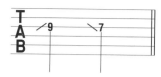

TRILL: Very rapidly alternate between the notes indicated by continuously hammering on and pulling off.

TAPPING: Hammer ("tap") the fret indicated with the pick-hand index or middle finger and pull off to the note fretted by the fret hand.

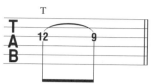

NATURAL HARMONIC: Strike the note while the fret-hand lightly touches the string directly over the fret indicated.

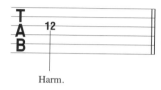

PINCH HARMONIC: The note is fretted normally and a harmonic is produced by adding the edge of the thumb or the tip of the index finger of the pick hand to the normal pick attack.

HARP HARMONIC: The note is fretted normally and a harmonic is produced by gently resting the pick hand's index finger directly above the indicated fret (in parentheses) while the pick hand's thumb or pick assists by plucking the appropriate string.

PICK SCRAPE: The edge of the pick is rubbed down (or up) the string, producing a scratchy sound.

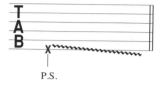

MUFFLED STRINGS: A percussive sound is produced by laying the fret hand across the string(s) without depressing, and striking them with the pick hand.

PALM MUTING: The note is partially muted by the pick hand lightly touching the string(s) just before the bridge.

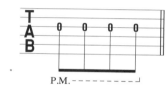

RAKE: Drag the pick across the strings indicated with a single motion.

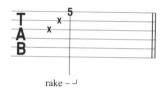

TREMOLO PICKING: The note is picked as rapidly and continuously as possible.

ARPEGGIATE: Play the notes of the chord indicated by quickly rolling them from bottom to top.

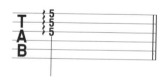

VIBRATO BAR DIVE AND RETURN: The pitch of the note or chord is dropped a specified number of steps (in rhythm), then returned to the original pitch.

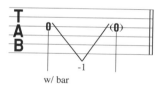

VIBRATO BAR SCOOP: Depress the bar just before striking the note, then quickly release the bar.

VIBRATO BAR DIP: Strike the note and then immediately drop a specified number of steps, then release back to the original pitch.

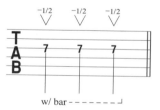

Additional Musical Definitions

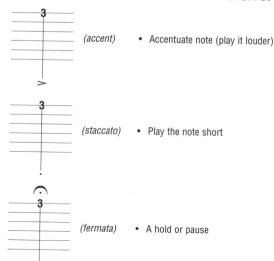

(accent)	• Accentuate note (play it louder)
(staccato)	• Play the note short
(fermata)	• A hold or pause

⊓	• Downstroke
V	• Upstroke
	• Repeat measures between signs

NOTE: Tablature numbers in parentheses are used when:
- The note is sustained, but a new articulation begins (such as a hammer-on, pull-off, slide, or bend), or
- A bend is released.
- A note sustains while crossing from one staff to another.

GUITAR RECORDED VERSIONS®

Guitar Recorded Versions® are note-for-note transcriptions of guitar music taken directly off recordings. This series, one of the most popular in print today, features some of the greatest guitar players and groups from blues and rock to country and jazz.

Guitar Recorded Versions are transcribed by the best transcribers in the business. Every book contains notes and tablature unless otherwise marked. Visit **www.halleonard.com** for our complete selection.